VOLUME 10

NEW TESTAMENT

THE NEW COLLEGEVILLE BIBLE COMMENTARY

JAMES
FIRST PETER
JUDE
SECOND PETER

Patrick J. Hartin

SERIES EDITOR

Daniel Durken, O.S.B.

LITURGICAL PRESS

Collegeville, Minnesota

www.litpress.org

hil obstat: Robert C. Harren, *Censor deputatus.*

primatur: ✠ John F. Kinney, Bishop of St. Cloud, Minnesota, December 29, 2005.

sign by Ann Blattner.

ver illustration: *Sermon on the Mount* by Donald Jackson. Natural hand-ground on calfskin vellum, 15-7/8" x 24-1/2". Copyright 2005 *The Saint John's Bible* and Hill Museum & Manuscript Library at Saint John's University, United States of America. Scripture quotations are from the New Revised Standard Version of the le, Catholic Edition, copyright © 1989, 1993 National Council of the Churches Christ in the United States of America. Used by permission. All rights reserved.

hotos: pages 6, 10, NOVA Photos; page 32, Corel Photos; pages 50, 60, Flat Earth 'hotos.

Scripture selections are taken from the New American Bible Copyright © 1991, 1986, 1970 by the Confraternity of Christian Doctrine, Inc., 3211 Fourth Street, NE, Washington, DC 20017-1194 and are used by license of the copyright owner. All rights reserved. No part of the New American Bible may be reproduced in any form or by any means without permission in writing from the copyright owner.

4	5	6	7	8	9

Library of Congress Cataloging-in-Publication Data

Hartin, P. J. (Patrick J.)
  James, First Peter, Jude, Second Peter / Patrick J. Hartin.
    p.   cm. — (The new Collegeville Bible commentary. New Testament ; v. 10)
  Summary: "Complete biblical texts with sound, scholarly based commentary that is written at a pastoral level; the Scripture translation is that of the New American Bible with Revised New Testament and Revised Psalms (1991)"—Provided by publisher.
    Includes bibliographical references.
    ISBN-13: 978-0-8146-2869-0 (pbk. : alk. paper)
    ISBN-10: 0-8146-2869-9 (pbk. : alk. paper)
  1. Bible. N.T. James—Commentaries. 2. Bible. N.T. Peter—Commentaries.
3. Bible. N.T. Jude—Commentaries. I. Title. II. Series.

BS2785.53.H372   2006
227'.9077—dc22

                                                          2005015549

CONTENTS

ABBREVIATIONS

Books of the Bible

Acts—Acts of the Apostles
Amos—Amos
Bar—Baruch
1 Chr—1 Chronicles
2 Chr—2 Chronicles
Col—Colossians
1 Cor—1 Corinthians
2 Cor—2 Corinthians
Dan—Daniel
Deut—Deuteronomy
Eccl (or Qoh)—Ecclesiastes
Eph—Ephesians
Esth—Esther
Exod—Exodus
Ezek—Ezekiel
Ezra—Ezra
Gal—Galatians
Gen—Genesis
Hab—Habakkuk
Hag—Haggai
Heb—Hebrews
Hos—Hosea
Isa—Isaiah
Jas—James
Jdt—Judith
Jer—Jeremiah
Job—Job
Joel—Joel
John—John
1 John—1 John
2 John—2 John
3 John—3 John
Jonah—Jonah
Josh—Joshua
Jude—Jude
Judg—Judges
1 Kgs—1 Kings

2 Kgs—2 Kings
Lam—Lamentations
Lev—Leviticus
Luke—Luke
1 Macc—1 Maccabees
2 Macc—2 Maccabees
Mal—Malachi
Mark—Mark
Matt—Matthew
Mic—Micah
Nah—Nahum
Neh—Nehemiah
Num—Numbers
Obad—Obadiah
1 Pet—1 Peter
2 Pet—2 Peter
Phil—Philippians
Phlm—Philemon
Prov—Proverbs
Ps(s)—Psalms
Rev—Revelation
Rom—Romans
Ruth—Ruth
1 Sam—1 Samuel
2 Sam—2 Samuel
Sir—Sirach
Song—Song of Songs
1 Thess—1 Thessalonians
2 Thess—2 Thessalonians
1 Tim—1 Timothy
2 Tim—2 Timothy
Titus—Titus
Tob—Tobit
Wis—Wisdom
Zech—Zechariah
Zeph—Zephaniah

THE GENERAL LETTERS

The term "catholic letters" has traditionally been used to designate a group of seven New Testament writings: James, 1 and 2 Peter, 1, 2, and 3 John, and Jude as distinct from the writings of Paul. In the Eastern church the word "catholic" (used in the sense of "universal") was applied to these seven writings. This was an outgrowth of the theological under-standing that they were writings addressed, not to any specific church, but to the church at large. This designation indicated the encyclical nature of the letter in that it was intended to be circulated among many churches. In the Western church the designation for these writings was "canonical epistles" *(epistolae canonicae)* indicating the idea that they were letters ap-proved for reading in the liturgy throughout the Christian world.

When Bishop Athanasius of Alexandria issued his Easter letter con-taining the list of New Testament books in A.D. 367, the catholic letters were placed immediately after the Acts of the Apostles and before the let-ters of Paul. This same order can be found in many ancient lists of the New Testament canon. It seems that this was the traditional order. The Codex Sinaiticus and the Latin Vulgate adopted a different order, with Paul's letters following the Acts of the Apostles and the catholic letters placed after Paul's writings. The very influential role that the Latin Vul-gate played ultimately established this sequence as the traditional one fol-lowed today.

The Letter of James

Author

The author identifies himself as "James" (Greek, *Iakōbos*), recalling the Hebrew name Jacob, father of the "twelve tribes of Israel." This name was very common in the biblical world. Three significant members of the early Christian community bore this name: James, son of Zebedee, apostle and brother of John (Mark 1:19), executed by Herod Agrippa about A.D. 44 (Acts 12:2); James, son of Alphaeus, also an apostle (Mark 3:18); and James, "brother of the Lord" (Gal 1:19).

Some information regarding the author can be deduced from the text: (a) *He is at home within the world of Judaism.* He makes great use of the Wisdom traditions of Israel. His thought betrays the concrete mentality of the Hebrew Scriptures rather than the abstract thinking of the Greek. (b) *He is also at home within the world of nascent Christianity.* He shows numerous relationships with the thought and traditions of the Gospels, particularly the Sermon on the Mount. (c) *He writes with the authority of a teacher* (3:1). (d) *He does not appear to be an apostle.* The letters of Paul and Peter carefully indicate their role as apostles in their opening greetings (1 Cor 1:1; 1 Pet 1:1). Instead, the author refers to himself as "a slave of God and of the Lord Jesus Christ" (1:1).

James, "the brother of the Lord" and head of the Jerusalem church, appears to fit best the picture of the author that emerges from the text. He was equally at home in the world of Judaism and the world of early Christianity. Paul indicates that this James was among those who were privileged to witness the risen Jesus (1 Cor 15:7). He exercised an important position within the early Christian community in Jerusalem (Acts 12:17). He was an influential figure at the Council of Jerusalem (A.D. 49). Paul refers to him as one of "the pillars" of the church (Gal 2:9). He remained leader of the Jerusalem church until his martyrdom in A.D. 62. The Jewish historian Josephus also mentions him.

7

Ruins of an ancient settlement

One major difficulty with this suggestion is *the excellent quality of the Greek*—it is among the best in the entire New Testament. Stylistically, the writer shows great finesse at using literary devices to make his argument succinctly. This demands someone well educated in Greek rhetorical skills.

The best way to harmonize the evidence is to understand the reference to James (1:1) as demonstrating the writer's desire to invoke James as the authority behind this letter. He must be someone who was closely associated with James. The writer sends this letter in James's name ("the brother of the Lord") shortly after James's death to encourage Jewish-Christian communities in the Diaspora (particularly in the area of Syria or northern Palestine) to hold on to his traditions and teachings and to remind them of the importance they have as "the firstfruits of his [God's] creatures" (1:18).

The term "brother of the Lord" has been variously interpreted in the Christian tradition (see discussion in Patrick J. Hartin, *James,* Sacra Pagina Series 14 [Collegeville: The Liturgical Press, 2003] 16–25). However, it is best to see the word "brother" as referring to a broader understanding of kinship (rather than to a physical brother of Jesus). For two reasons: First, degrees of kinship were more loosely defined in the ancient world than they are today. (See, for example, John the Baptist's condemnation of Herod Antipas: "It is not lawful for you to have your *brother's* wife" [Mark 6:16; see also Luke 3:19]. Here, Herod Antipas was only the *step-brother* of Herod Philip.) Second, the above argument supports the Catholic tradition that Mary remained a virgin after giving birth to Jesus.

It is in this sense that this commentary refers to the author as "James, the brother of the Lord."

Hearers/readers

The text identifies the hearers/readers very graphically: "to the twelve tribes in the dispersion" (1:1). The best understanding of this phrase emerges from the hope for the restoration of the twelve-tribe kingdom of Israel. The Exile marked the beginning of the *dispersion* of the people of Israel, and the word "dispersion" (or *Diaspora*) became a technical term for those Israelites living outside Palestine. During the Exile the prophets proclaimed the restoration of this twelve-tribe kingdom. This became a central conviction in late Jewish eschatology and apocalyptic literature. It also lies behind Jesus' call to repentance (Matt 4:17). In Matthew 15:24 Jesus countered the appeal of the Syrophoenician woman with these words: "I was sent only to the lost sheep of the house of Israel." This passage conveys Jesus' mission as gathering in and reconstituting the twelve-tribe kingdom of Israel.

In addressing his hearers/readers in this way, James describes his task as similar to that of Jesus. They constitute the beginning of the restoration of the house of Israel. In line with 1:18, James sees that those who now belong to the new Israel are the "firstfruits" and represent a foretaste of the future, final restoration of God's people.

Genre and purpose

The letter of James belongs to the general class of Wisdom literature that proliferated throughout Israel and the ancient Near East in the first two centuries B.C. While Martin Dibelius classified James as *paraenesis* (a collection of moral exhortations), some modern scholars have proposed that it should be viewed more precisely as *protreptic discourse,* that is, a discourse containing sustained arguments that strive to develop a theme more thoroughly. Since the purpose of protreptic discourse is that of *social formation,* James aims at reminding his hearers/readers of those values that give them their identity as the twelve-tribe kingdom and separate them from the wider society.

Major themes

While the name of Jesus occurs only twice (1:1; 2:1), references to God are far more numerous. The concept of God is at home in the world and belief of Judaism in the first century A.D. In line with the Jewish profession of faith, God is one (2:19). God is merciful and compassionate (5:11); the Father of lights, the creator of the world (1:17); the champion of the poor (5:1-6); and the lawgiver and the judge (4:12; 5:9).

James's message calls believers to harmonize their faith and action. James's ethic was not meant to be read in an individualistic sense, but rather in a communitarian way. James lies squarely in the tradition of the prophets before him in giving expression to the voice of the poor and the marginalized in society. In line with Jesus' teaching, James promises the poor the inheritance of the kingdom (Jas 2:5; Luke 6:20) and challenges the conscience of every hearer/reader to respect the poor.

The Letter of James

I. Address

1 ¹James, a slave of God and of the Lord Jesus Christ, to the twelve tribes in the dispersion, greetings.

II. The Value of Trials and Temptation

Perseverance in Trial. ²Consider it all joy, my brothers, when you encounter various trials, ³for you know that the testing of your faith produces perseverance. ⁴And let perseverance be perfect, so that you may be perfect and complete, lacking in nothing. ⁵But if any of you lacks wisdom, he should ask God who gives to all generously and ungrudgingly, and he will be given it. ⁶But he should ask in faith, not doubting, for the one who doubts is like a wave of the

1:1 Greetings

This opening follows the usual structure of a first-century letter by mentioning the author, those to whom it is written, and concluding with greetings. The writer identifies himself simply as James. Since he does not identify himself further, the reader associates him with the most important James in the early church, the leader of the church in Jerusalem, "James, the brother of the Lord" (see Introduction, pp. 7–8). Rather than speak from above, the author chooses the term "slave of God," which recalls the long biblical tradition that identifies leaders of the people in this way, such as Moses (1 Kgs 8:53), David (1 Kgs 8:66), and the prophets (Jer 7:25). It is used in the sense of obedience to God's will and loyalty to God's service (see also Phil 2:7; 1 Pet 2:16).

The community to whom the author writes is identified as "the twelve tribes in the dispersion." By this term the readers are described as the fulfillment of Israel's hopes in the restoration of God's twelve-tribe kingdom in the eschatological age. The long-awaited hopes of the past are now being realized with these Christian communities that are emerging from

▶ This symbol indicates a cross reference number in the *Catechism of the Catholic Church*. See page 76 for number citations.

A ramshackle animal's shelter in Jerusalem

sea that is driven and tossed about by the wind. ⁷For that person must not suppose that he will receive anything from the Lord, ⁸since he is a man of two minds, unstable in all his ways.

⁹The brother in lowly circumstances should take pride in his high standing, ¹⁰and the rich one in his lowliness, for he will pass away "like the flower of the field." ¹¹For the sun comes up with its scorching heat and dries up the grass, its flower droops, and the beauty of its appearance vanishes. So will the rich person fade away in the midst of his pursuits.

Temptation. ¹²Blessed is the man who perseveres in temptation, for when he has been proved he will receive the crown of life that he promised to those who love him. ¹³No one experiencing ▶

---

the people of Israel. The word "dispersion" (literally, Diaspora) means "scattering" and refers to those areas outside Palestine where the people of Israel had been scattered (see Deut 30:4; Neh 1:9; see Introduction, p. 8). Undoubtedly, James is writing to Jewish Christians, who see their community as the beginning of these hopes, for they are the "firstfruits" (1:18). The author intends to outline the type of life this newly constituted Israel is called to embrace. This writing helps readers of every age to see themselves as true heirs of Israel's traditions. He uses the standard form of "greeting" that opens Greco-Roman letters *(chairein)*. He deliberately uses this brief greeting in order to connect with the word for "joy" *(charan)* in the next verse. This is part of James's style of using catchphrases to develop the letter.

1:2-11 Testing, wisdom and the lowly

In place of the traditional thanksgiving section that characterized a Pauline letter, the letter of James introduces two sections expressing joy (1:2-11) and blessing (1:12-27), which present the major themes that will unfold throughout the letter.

The first introductory section (1:2-11) begins with a call to the community to *"consider it all joy"* (1:2; emphasis added) when they experience *the testing of their faith* (1:2-4, *the first theme*). Faith is as important for James as it is for Paul, occurring some sixteen times in this short letter (1:3, 6; 2:1, 5, 14[twice], 17, 18[three times], 20, 22[twice], 24, 26; 5:15). Whenever believers, individually or as a group, are involved in the ordeal of suffering, they should accept it joyfully. As gold is tested and purified by fire, so believers will be purified by trials. Testing produces steadfastness, which in turn leads to wholeness or integrity *(perfection,* 1:3-4). It reminds the reader of Matthew's Jesus in the Sermon on the Mount exhorting his hearers: "So be perfect, just as your heavenly Father is perfect" (Matt 5:48).

temptation should say, "I am being tempted by God"; for God is not subject to temptation to evil, and he himself tempts no one. ¹⁴Rather, each person is tempted when he is lured and enticed by his own desire. ¹⁵Then desire conceives and brings forth sin, and when sin reaches maturity it gives birth to death.

¹⁶Do not be deceived, my beloved brothers: ¹⁷all good giving and every perfect gift is from above, coming down from the Father of lights, with whom there is no alteration or shadow caused by change. ¹⁸He willed to give us birth by the word of truth that we may be a kind of firstfruits of his creatures.

A second theme emerges in 1:5-8 with the request for wisdom. In the biblical traditions God is the source of all wisdom: "The beginning of wisdom is the fear of the LORD" (Prov 9:10). The gift of wisdom enables people to act in the midst of trials so that their actions lead to wholeness (*perfection*). "Indeed, though one be perfect among the sons of men, / if Wisdom, who comes from you, be not with him, / he shall be held in no esteem" (Wis 9:6). Wisdom is that one gift needed for perfection understood as wholeness, completion, and integrity. James instructs his hearers/readers that if they lack wisdom, they are to ask God, for God is the only one who can grant it. This is similar to the command of Jesus, "Ask and it will be given to you" (Matt 7:7). The believer must pray to God for wisdom, for the knowledge of how to act correctly. For James the root cause of unanswered prayer is lack of faith in God. One is "of two minds" (1:8), having a divided loyalty, as Jesus indicates in Matthew's Sermon on the Mount: "No one can serve two masters. . . . You cannot serve God and mammon" (Matt 6:24). This is a central theme for James, who calls on his readers to make a choice between friendship with God and friendship with the world (4:4).

James introduces a third theme here that has importance throughout the letter, namely, *the contrast between rich and poor* (1:9-11). Both the poor and rich are called upon to "take pride" or to boast in what God does for them. The background for this concept of boasting lies in the Hebrew Scriptures, where God is the source of all blessings (see Jer 9:22-23). The lowly are to rejoice because God has given them an exalted status within the Christian community, where they experience equality with one another. The rich, on the other hand, are those who have lost their position within the wider community, only to discover a true status within the Christian community. True humility finds favor with God (see Sir 3:18). The rich recognize the fragility of life: those who place confidence in their own "pursuits" will waste away suddenly like a wild flower burnt up by the scorching heat (1:11).

III. Exhortations
and Warnings

Doers of the Word. [19]Know this, my dear brothers: everyone should be quick to hear, slow to speak, slow to wrath, [20]for the wrath of a man does not accomplish the righteousness of God. [21]Therefore, put away all filth and evil excess and humbly welcome the word that has been planted in you and is able to save your souls.

1:12-27 Testing, hearers and doers of the word

A second introductory section, introduced with the word "Blessed," again announces major themes that will be taken up in the body of the letter. The first theme expressed here (*endurance under testing brings with it the crown of life,* 1:12-18) is parallel to the first theme of the previous section. Essentially James is saying: "Blessed is the person who withstands trial; that person is progressing toward salvation" (1:12). This is similar to the Beatitudes described in Matthew 5:3-12. James wishes to emphasize that present trials will effect their reward ("the crown of life," 1:12), because such trials give believers the chance to show their love for God.

The trials that are experienced are not to be regarded as temptations sent by God (1:13). The Gospel tradition holds that temptations do not come from God but from the devil (e.g., Jesus' temptations in the Synoptic Gospels). James continues in the same tradition. The truth is that people are tempted by desires that entice them. The consequence of desiring is described in terms of the image of giving birth (1:14-15): when desire conceives, it gives birth to sin; and when it is fully mature, it gives birth to death in its turn.

James's image of God emerges clearly from this section. God is not the source of evil but the origin of everything that is good (1:16-17). James describes God as the "Father of lights" (1:17). Unlike the heavenly bodies, whose movements result in variations of the light they send out, their creator, God, is unchanging. God's love for humanity is always constant. God's greatest gifts to humanity have been those of creation and rebirth as "the firstfruits of his [God's] creatures" (1:18). This connects back to the opening of the letter to "the twelve tribes in the dispersion." God's gift of rebirth is meant to encompass all humanity: the first implies that others will follow.

A series of sayings brings this introductory section to a conclusion (1:19-27): be slow to anger (1:20-21); quick to hear (1:22-25); and slow to speak (1:26-27). They contain wisdom advice for the hearer/reader on how to lead life in order to be counted among those who are blessed. The hearers/readers are admonished first of all to be *"slow to wrath"* (1:19; emphasis added), because human anger does not conform to God's righteousness, the moral

²²Be doers of the word and not hearers only, deluding yourselves. ²³For if anyone is a hearer of the word and not a doer, he is like a man who looks at his own face in a mirror. ²⁴He sees himself, then goes off and promptly forgets what he looked like. ²⁵But the one who peers into the perfect law of freedom and perseveres, and is not a hearer who forgets but a doer who acts, such a one shall be blessed in what he does.

²⁶If anyone thinks he is religious and does not bridle his tongue but deceives his heart, his religion is vain. ²⁷Religion

---

standards set by God. "The word that has been planted in you" (1:21) refers to the word of the gospel that was implanted in the hearts of the believers when they came to rebirth as God's creatures. They are to welcome this word by putting it into practice in their lives. For James salvation requires a response on the part of the believer that is demonstrated in action led according to the moral standards set by God.

Next, James takes up his call to "be quick to hear" (1:19; emphasis added), which focuses on putting faith into action: *"Be doers of the word and not hearers only"* (1:22; emphasis added). This phrase is a suitable summary of the whole letter, expressing the central call to the believer. The word is God's will expressed also in the biblical law (or Torah). The word of the gospel, the message of Jesus, the biblical law—these are all expressions for God's word, God's moral law for God's people. They are different stages of the same reality. Jesus' message captures the heart of the biblical law in the "royal law . . . 'You shall love your neighbor as yourself'" (2:8). James illustrates his call to put faith into action by means of a brief parable. The point is captured in 1:24: those who do not follow God's word in their lives 'are like those who glance briefly at themselves in a mirror and immediately forget what they looked like.

Finally, the saying "be slow to speak" (1:19; emphasis added) is taken up in 1:26-27. In effect, James says: "If you think you are religious but you lack control of speech, you deceive yourselves and your religion is worthless." James is concerned with the inconsistency between belief and speech and returns to this theme elsewhere throughout this letter (2:14-17; 3:9-10; 4:3). This leads him to provide a definition of religion in terms of action (1:27). It is expressed first in terms of caring for widows and orphans. Believers are called upon to imitate God in their actions. The community shows its true relationship with God by reaching out to the least members of society. *Orphans and widows* were symbolic for the most unfortunate members and a reminder of God's care for their community in the past: "You shall not violate the rights of the alien or of the orphan, nor take the clothing of a widow as a pledge. For, remember, you were once slaves in Egypt, and the LORD,

that is pure and undefiled before God and the Father is this: to care for orphans and widows in their affliction and to keep oneself unstained by the world.

2 **Sins of Partiality.** [1]My brothers, show no partiality as you adhere to the faith in our glorious Lord Jesus Christ. [2]For if a man with gold rings on his fingers and in fine clothes comes into your assembly, and a poor person in shabby clothes also comes in, [3]and you pay attention to the one wearing the fine clothes and say, "Sit here, please," while you say to the poor one, "Stand there," or "Sit at my feet," [4]have you not made

---

your God, ransomed you from there; that is why I command you to observe this rule" (Deut 24:17-18; see also Exod 22:20-23; Ps 94:1-23). The affliction of orphans and widows came from their lack of protection and legal status when the head of the family died. James adds a further identifying marker for his community: religious people should also keep themselves from the defilement of the world (1:27). The call is made not to be conformed to the standards of this world but to take one's values from the gospel message, which continues God's will as expressed in the biblical Torah.

Five themes from this introductory section will be explored throughout the letter: endurance through trial (1:2-4; 12-18; 5:7-11); asking for wisdom (1:5-8; 3:13-18; 4:1-10); the contrast of rich and poor (1:9-11; 2:1-13; 5:1-6); being doers of the word (1:22-25; 2:14-26; 4:13-17); and control of the tongue (1:26-27; 3:1-12; 4:11-12).

2:1-13 Do not show favoritism

James begins the body of the letter by taking up the theme of the contrast between rich and poor introduced before (1:9-11). He envisages a context in which the rich exploit their positions to oppress the powerless. Discrimination against people is incompatible with the faith of Jesus Christ. This is the second of only two explicit references to Jesus in the letter (1:1). The phrase "faith in our glorious Lord Jesus Christ" is difficult to translate. Literally it reads: "the faith of our Lord Jesus Christ of the glory." In referring to the "faith of our Lord Jesus Christ," James refers to Jesus' faithfulness to the Father's will through the obedience of his life. Jesus' faithfulness becomes an example for all believers. In the letter of James faith is directed toward the Father rather than toward Jesus (see 2:19, 23).

James goes on to paint a vivid picture of discrimination: favoritism shown to the rich at the expense of the poor (2:2-4). Even worse, this discrimination is within the assembly, where it ought not occur. James calls the gathering place of Christians an "assembly" (literally, "synagogue," 2:2). The choice of the word "synagogue" in preference to the more customary Christian designation of *ekklesia* is interesting. This is the only time

distinctions among yourselves and become judges with evil designs?

⁵Listen, my beloved brothers. Did not God choose those who are poor in the world to be rich in faith and heirs of the kingdom that he promised to those who love him? ⁶But you dishonored the poor person. Are not the rich oppressing you? And do they themselves not haul you off to court? ⁷Is it not they who blaspheme the noble name that was invoked over you? ⁸However, if you fulfill the royal law according to the scripture, "You shall love your neighbor as yourself," you are doing well. ⁹But if you show partiality, you commit sin, and are convicted by the law as transgressors. ¹⁰For whoever keeps the whole

in the New Testament where a Christian gathering is identified as a "synagogue," indicating the closeness of James's community to its roots within the world of Israel.

James provides an example of such atrocious behavior that every reader has to concur that this is not the way the community should behave as followers of Jesus (2:2-4). In a sense, James challenges the accepted values of his own world, in which honor is bestowed upon the rich and powerful. This example also challenges every succeeding generation to reevaluate its own treatment of people and to root out every form of discrimination. Indirectly, James reminds them of Jesus' teaching: the poor are promised the inheritance of the kingdom (2:5; see Matt 5:3).

James provides further support for his call not to discriminate in 2:5-13. He begins by providing an argument based upon God's actions: God has chosen "the poor in the world to be rich in faith and heirs of the kingdom" (2:5). Discrimination also transgresses the royal law, namely, "You shall love your neighbor as yourself" (2:8). James insists that those who belong to a community guided by "the royal law" of love cannot discriminate. The law of love is the true law guiding every aspect of life. Just as Jesus presented the law of love as the epitome of the law itself (see Matt 22:36-40), so James sees it fulfilling the same role. To discriminate breaks Jesus' command to love and makes one a transgressor of the law (2:9). One is called on to carry out the whole law (2:10-11).

Jesus' teaching in the Sermon on the Mount upholds the same vision of carrying out the whole law: "Do not think that I have come to abolish the law or the prophets. I have come not to abolish but to fulfill. Amen, I say to you, until heaven and earth pass away, not the smallest letter or the smallest part of a letter will pass from the law, until all things have taken place" (Matt 5:17-18). This is not casuistry, but rather an understanding of what the law (Torah) is all about. The law (Torah) is the expression of

law, but falls short in one particular, has become guilty in respect to all of it. ¹¹For he who said, "You shall not commit adultery," also said, "You shall not kill." Even if you do not commit adultery but kill, you have become a transgressor of the law. ¹²So speak and so act as people who will be judged by the law of freedom. ¹³For the judgment is merciless to one who has not shown mercy; mercy triumphs over judgment.

Faith and Works. ¹⁴What good is it, my brothers, if someone says he has faith but does not have works? Can that faith save him? ¹⁵If a brother or sister has nothing to wear and has no food for the day, ¹⁶and one of you says to them, "Go in peace, keep warm, and eat well," but you do not give them the necessities of the body, what good is it? ¹⁷So also faith of itself, if it does not have works, is dead.

God's will for humanity. One's whole life must be orientated toward implementing God's will completely.

James's thought concludes with an expression of general principles of judgment and mercy (2:12-13). Mercy triumphs over judgment: for those who have practiced mercy, there is no need to fear judgment (see Jesus' parable on the judgment of the nations, Matt 25:31-46).

2:14-26 Doers of the word / faith and works

This passage continues the line of thought of the previous passage (2:1-13), in which James had stressed that an imitation of Jesus' faithfulness (2:1) excluded discrimination against others. Now, in 2:14-26, this same faith is examined more fully, especially insofar as it expresses itself in action. He presents the theme of the whole argument in 2:14. Faith that is alive needs to demonstrate itself in action—that is the type of faith that saves. In the style of a Greek diatribe, James uses an imaginary example to illustrate the type of faith that saves (2:15-17). On its own faith without works is dead.

James describes a situation in which a living faith will manifest itself in appropriate deeds. His illustration of a brother or sister lacking clothing or food is reminiscent of the parable of the judgment of the nations in Matthew 25:31-46. James concludes with a brief summary of what he had stated in the opening thesis (2:14): faith without works is dead (2:17). He repeats the same refrain again in 2:26. By way of offering proof for his argument, James invents an imaginary opponent to whom he issues the challenge: "Demonstrate your faith to me without works" (2:18). The implication in this challenge is that of course he cannot. Then James offers to show him his faith from his works (2:18). The very heart of the Jewish profession of faith in God as one (the *Shema Israel* expressed in Deuteronomy 6:4-5) required a response in active love. Jesus stressed the same concept

¹⁸Indeed someone may say, "You have faith and I have works." Demonstrate your faith to me without works, and I will demonstrate my faith to you from my works. ¹⁹You believe that God is one. You do well. Even the demons believe that and tremble. ²⁰Do you want proof, you ignoramus, that faith without works is useless? ²¹Was not Abraham our father justified by works when he offered his son Isaac upon the altar? ²²You see that faith was active

that this profession of faith needed to be demonstrated in love of neighbor (Matt 22:36-40). James continues these traditions by showing that true faith needs a response of love (2:18-19); otherwise it is a dead faith, in the same category as the faith of the demons, who believe that God is one "and tremble" (2:19).

To support his perspective (2:20-25), James turns to the Scriptures. Abraham's exemplary behavior is used to support his thesis that good works are necessary. The choice of the example of Abraham is deliberate. As the forefather of Israel, he is also the father of James's community as heir of Israel's traditions. Abraham was justified not by faith alone but rather through his works, seen especially in his willingness to offer his beloved son Isaac on the altar. A conclusion is drawn from the scriptural reference. What was true in the case of Abraham is true universally (2:24): faith unaccompanied by works is not genuine. Abraham is characterized here as "the friend of God" (2:23). This is significant because James wishes to draw a sharp distinction between those who seek friendship with God and those who find friendship with the world (see 4:4 and the comment on 1:8).

In addition to the holy patriarch, James gives a further example from the Scriptures of someone whose faith flowed forth into works, namely, the prostitute Rahab (2:25). Matthew's early Christian traditions held her in high regard, as can be seen through her incorporation into the genealogy in Matthew's Gospel as an ancestor of Jesus (Matt 1:5). Her hospitality to the messengers of God's people is held up for imitation. She exemplified what James said earlier about caring for widows and orphans (1:27). Christian congregations ought to receive representatives of the church in the same way. Rahab becomes a type of the Christian congregation. James finally clinches his basic thesis with a statement that harks back to the opening of this passage (2:14, as well as to 2:17): "just as a body without a spirit is dead, so also faith without works is dead" (2:26).

Most attention in the letter of James has been focused on this passage because of its seeming conflict with Paul's thought regarding the relationship between faith and works. However, James and Paul are considering two very different issues. James is speaking about *works of faith*, whereas

along with his works, and faith was completed by the works. [23]Thus the scripture was fulfilled that says, "Abraham believed God, and it was credited to him as righteousness," and he was called "the friend of God." [24]See how a person is justified by works and not by faith alone. [25]And in the same way, was not Rahab the harlot also justified by works when she welcomed the messengers and sent them out by a different route? [26]For just as a body without a spirit is dead, so also faith without works is dead.

3 Power of the Tongue. [1]Not many of you should become teachers, my brothers, for you realize that we will be judged more strictly, [2]for we all fall short in many respects. If anyone does not fall short in speech, he is a perfect man, able to bridle his whole body also. [3]If we put bits into the mouths of horses to make them obey us, we also guide their whole bodies. [4]It is the same with ships: even though they are so large and driven by fierce winds, they are steered by a very small rudder wherever the pilot's inclination wishes. [5]In

Paul has in mind *works of the law* (Rom 3:28). James's focus is on living out faith in action: "Be doers of the word and not hearers only" (1:22). Faith needs to demonstrate through works that it is alive. Paul, on the other hand, was concerned with a different issue, namely, the question of how one arrives at faith: not through the Jewish law, but through God's free gift. Paul was contrasting *faith with the law*, while James was contrasting *an active faith with a dead faith.*

3:1-12 The tongue and speech

Chapter 3 turns attention to the teacher and the wise person. Once again James takes up themes mentioned in the introductory sections. In the spirit of the Wisdom literature, James gives advice on how to lead life in harmony with faith. An admonition on not becoming a teacher forms the introduction to the discussion on the tongue (3:1). This consideration is particularly appropriate for the role of a teacher within the community. Teaching was exercised chiefly through the oral word of instruction rather than through the written word. The teacher's role in the early church was vital for the development and growth of the community. It could be either positive (building up the community) or negative (undermining or destroying the community).

The role of teachers is often mentioned in the early church (see Acts 13:1; 1 Cor 12:28; Eph 4:11). Teachers focused attention on guiding the community to remain true to their traditions, while showing how these traditions could be newly interpreted and applied to the new situations of the Christian communities. In speaking of the teacher, James does not

the same way the tongue is a small member and yet has great pretensions.

Consider how small a fire can set a huge forest ablaze. ⁶The tongue is also a fire. It exists among our members as a world of malice, defiling the whole body and setting the entire course of our lives on fire, itself set on fire by Gehenna. ⁷For every kind of beast and bird, of reptile and sea creature, can be tamed and has been tamed by the human species, ⁸but no human being can tame the tongue. It is a restless evil, full of deadly poison. ⁹With it we bless the Lord and Father, and with it we curse human beings who are made in the likeness of God. ¹⁰From the same mouth come blessing and cursing. This need not be so, my brothers. ¹¹Does a spring gush forth from the same opening both pure and brackish water? ¹²Can a fig tree, my brothers, produce olives, or a grapevine figs? Neither can salt water yield fresh.

---

have an office in mind, but rather a function that is being exercised. James himself functions as a teacher for his community in that he endeavors to apply the Torah and Jesus' teachings to the situation of his own community. For James, the reason people should not become teachers is that "we all fall short in many respects"—in other words, "all of us make many mistakes" (3:2). This theme is common in Hellenistic writings and is also found in the Scriptures (Sir 19:15; Eccl 7:20; 1 John 1:8 and 10). Only "the perfect [person]" (3:2) is able to control speech.

Once again James introduces the theme of perfection or wholeness (see 1:4; 1:25; 2:22). The believer strives for wholeness or integrity in every dimension of life, including speech. James adds image to image, building up the picture of the evil perpetrated by the unguarded tongue (3:3-5a). Like the charioteer, who controls a horse through a small bit, or the pilot, who guides the ship by means of a tiny rudder, so the small tongue controls and guides the whole body, for good or evil. Using language derived from philosophy that had become part of popular culture, James speaks of the evil influence that the tongue exercises on human life at every stage of its development (3:6). James concludes pessimistically that "no human being can tame the tongue" (3:8).

The letter further develops the dangers of the tongue (3:5b-10) by using two frightening images: the tongue is a fire, and the tongue is a cosmic force (3:6). The tongue of the natural, unredeemed person cannot be tamed; it is a "restless evil, full of deadly poison" (3:8). James goes on to speak of the contradictory work of the tongue: we bless God and curse one another (3:9-12). To bless God is the greatest function of the human tongue: thrice daily the devout Jew praised God. But at the same time this tongue is used to curse one another. James emphasizes that the person

21

True Wisdom. [13]Who among you is wise and understanding? Let him show his works by a good life in the humility that comes from wisdom. [14]But if you have bitter jealousy and selfish ambition in your hearts, do not boast and be false to the truth. [15]Wisdom of this kind does not come down from above but is earthly, unspiritual, demonic. [16]For where jealousy and selfish ambition exist, there is disorder and every foul practice. [17]But the wisdom from above

---

who is the object of the curse "is made in the likeness of God" (3:9). Consequently, the curse is directed at God.

3:13–4:10 Call to friendship with God

A feature of ancient instruction was the use of what is termed a *topos,* that is, the systematic development of a theme or topic in a standard way. Two such *topoi* lie behind James's instruction: the *topos* of speech (in the previous passage, 3:1-12) and the *topos* of envy (in the present passage, 3:13–4:10). For this reason 3:13–4:10 is judged to be a single unit as it deals clearly and systematically with the topic of envy. Attention now shifts from the teacher to the wise person. This section opens with the rhetorical question: "Who among you is wise and understanding?" (3:13) and introduces the argument that a believer's whole life must demonstrate works/deeds that are inspired by wisdom from above (3:13).

True disciples know that it is characteristic of truly righteous persons to be inspired by divine wisdom. In this way they show dependence on God. James illustrates a twofold lifestyle for his readers: the one is led without the wisdom from above and is characterized by a life full of "bitter jealousy and selfish ambition" (3:14), which is "earthly, unspiritual, demonic" (3:15). In contrast to this "non-wisdom," James sketches a lifestyle influenced by true wisdom from above (3:17): it is "pure, peaceable, gentle, compliant, full of mercy and good fruits, without inconstancy or insincerity" (3:17). Jesus taught in Matthew's Sermon on the Mount that "by their fruits you will know them" (Matt 7:16). Genuine believers will always exhibit wisdom by the kind of life they lead, which will bring them righteousness (3:18).

James continues to expand the argument by developing this *topos* of envy (jealousy) in 4:1-10. His reference to conflicts and wars (4:1) is characteristic of this *topos* of envy. James is not saying that wars and conflicts have occurred within his community. Instead, he is using a rhetorical device to draw attention to the consequences of envy. James 4:2 is a difficult verse to translate. The New Revised Standard Version (NRSV) offers a

is first of all pure, then peaceable, gentle, compliant, full of mercy and good fruits, without inconstancy or insincerity. [18]And the fruit of righteousness is sown in peace for those who cultivate peace.

4 Causes of Division. [1]Where do the wars and where do the conflicts among you come from? Is it not from your passions that make war within your members? [2]You covet but do not possess. You kill and envy but you cannot obtain; you fight and wage war. You do not possess because you do not ask. [3]You ask but do not receive, because you ask wrongly, to spend it on your passions. [4]Adulterers! Do you not know that to be a lover of the world means enmity with God? Therefore, whoever wants to be a lover of the world makes himself an enemy of God. [5]Or do you suppose that the scripture speaks without meaning when it says, "The spirit that he has made to dwell in us tends toward jealousy"? [6]But he bestows a greater grace; therefore, it says:

"God resists the proud,
but gives grace to the humble."

---

more logical option than the New American Bible (NAB): "You want something and do not have it; so you commit murder. And you covet something and cannot obtain it; so you engage in disputes and conflicts." The reason for preferring this translation to the NAB comes from the reference "You kill (murder)." In the NAB translation (see text above) this phrase stands on its own, whereas in the NRSV translation it is understood as a consequence of the inordinate desire of envy, which is the main theme of this whole section.

The heart of James's letter occurs in 4:4 with the contrast drawn between friendship with the world and friendship with God. A choice is given to the hearer/reader: you have to decide between friendship with God or with the world. This reaches back to the opening of the letter (1:8), where reference was made to the "man of two minds." Jesus offers the same choice in the Sermon on the Mount: "You cannot serve God and mammon" (Matt 6:24). The opening word of 4:4 ("Adulterers") underscores the seriousness of this choice, since it recalls breaking the covenant relationship between God and God's people. Throughout the Hebrew Scriptures the breaking of the covenant relationship is compared to the rupture of the marriage bond through adultery.

As he has done previously, James offers two scriptural quotations to support his argument. The first quotation (4:5) is difficult to identify: "The spirit that he has made to dwell in us tends toward jealousy." Probably James is quoting a text from memory, which makes identification difficult. James adds a second quotation: "God resists the proud, / but gives grace to the humble" (4:6, which comes from Proverbs 3:34).

⁷So submit yourselves to God. Resist the devil, and he will flee from you. ⁸Draw near to God, and he will draw near to you. Cleanse your hands, you sinners, and purify your hearts, you of two minds. ⁹Begin to lament, to mourn, to weep. Let your laughter be turned into mourning and your joy into dejection. ¹⁰Humble yourselves before the Lord and he will exalt you.

¹¹Do not speak evil of one another, brothers. Whoever speaks evil of a brother or judges his brother speaks evil of the law and judges the law. If you judge the law, you are not a doer of the law but a judge. ¹²There is one law-

From discussing the causes of strife, James turns attention to its remedies (4:7-10). One is asked to submit to God and to resist the devil (4:7). The call to "cleanse your hands . . . and purify your hearts" (4:8) symbolizes a call to pay attention to both actions ("hands") and thoughts ("hearts"). See Sirach 38:10: "Let your hands be just, / cleanse your heart of every sin." "You of two minds" (4:8) again refers to 1:8 and 4:4: you cannot vacillate in allegiance to God. James concludes his argument (4:10) with a saying that is reminiscent of the Jesus saying: "Whoever exalts himself will be humbled; but whoever humbles himself will be exalted" (Matt 23:12; see Luke 14:11; 18:14). Humility is not a social condition but a moral and spiritual one.

4:11-12 Speaking evil against another

For the third time James returns to the theme of speech (see 1:26; 3:1-12). Those who set themselves over against their brothers and sisters by criticizing and judging them also speak against the law and pass judgment on the law. Jesus utters similar instructions not to judge another in the Sermon on the Mount (Matt 7:1). Slander is a serious breach of the command to love one's neighbor (2:8; see also Lev 19:16-18). God is the lawgiver, and humanity is called to be a doer of the law. The concept of God as lawgiver and judge is fundamental to the Hebrew Scriptures. Humanity must be careful not to usurp God's role. James sums up the argument with a rhetorical question: "Who then are you to judge your neighbor?" (4:12). Paul asks a similar question in Romans 14:4: "Who are you to pass judgment on someone else's servant?"

4:13–5:6 Judgment on the rich because of friendship with the world

Here James reflects on a major theme in this letter: the choice between friendship with the world and friendship with God. Two examples (4:13-17; 5:1-6) show how a choice for the world leads to certain consequences. James returns to the theme of the rich for the final time (see 1:9-11; 2:1-13). Merchants are viewed as examples of those who seek friendship with the world (4:13-17). James condemns them for their presumption in laying

giver and judge who is able to save or to destroy. Who then are you to judge your neighbor?

Warning against Presumption. [13]Come now, you who say, "Today or tomorrow we shall go into such and such a town, spend a year there doing business, and make a profit"— [14]you have no idea what your life will be like tomorrow. You are a puff of smoke that appears briefly and then disappears. [15]Instead you should say, "If the Lord wills it, we shall live to do this or that." [16]But now you are boasting in your arrogance. All such boasting is evil. [17]So for one who knows the right thing to do and does not do it, it is a sin.

5 **Warning to the Rich.** [1]Come now, you rich, weep and wail over your impending miseries. [2]Your wealth has rotted away, your clothes have become moth-eaten, [3]your gold and silver have corroded, and that corrosion will be a testimony against you; it will devour your flesh like a fire. You have stored up treasure for the last days. [4]Behold, the wages you withheld from the workers who harvested your fields are crying aloud, and the cries of the harvesters have reached the ears of the Lord of

---

plans without any reference to God or God's will (4:15). James concludes with a statement that implies responsibility for one's actions (4:17).

In 5:1-6 James changes focus from merchants to the rich, landowning class. When James calls upon the rich to "weep and wail over your impending miseries" (5:1), he is not addressing them (the rich) directly, but his own community. As with the prophets before him, this exhortation is intended to encourage the hearers/readers to remain faithful by showing what is about to befall those outside the community (namely the rich).

James's first attack is against the substance of the rich persons' wealth: it is valueless (5:2-3). In mentioning the coming misfortunes, the author presents them as having already occurred: their garments are damaged; their gold and silver have been destroyed. Matthew 6:19-20 (Luke 12:33-34) presents an interesting parallel to this text: "Do not store up for yourselves treasures on earth, where moth and decay destroy, and thieves break in and steal. But store up treasures in heaven, where neither moth nor decay destroys, nor thieves break in and steal. For where your treasure is, there also will your heart be."

James levels three accusations against the rich: they have defrauded the day-laborers out of their just wage (5:4); they have lived their lives in luxury and self-indulgence; and they have brought the innocent or "righteous one" into court for trial, so that he has been condemned (5:6). Once again the rejection of God's power forms the basic indictment James levels against the rich. They have made a choice for friendship with the world and have usurped everything to suit their own prosperity. The rich have yet to discover and experience the reality of God's power acting on behalf

25

hosts. [5]You have lived on earth in luxury and pleasure; you have fattened your hearts for the day of slaughter. [6]You have condemned; you have murdered the righteous one; he offers you no resistance.

Patience and Oaths. [7]Be patient, therefore, brothers, until the coming of the Lord. See how the farmer waits for the precious fruit of the earth, being patient with it until it receives the early and the late rains. [8]You too must be patient. Make your hearts firm, because the coming of the Lord is at hand. [9]Do not complain, brothers, about one another, that you may not be judged. Behold, the Judge is standing before the gates. [10]Take as an example of hardship and patience, brothers, the prophets who spoke in the name of the Lord. [11]Indeed we call blessed those who have persevered. You have heard of the

---

of the poor and oppressed (5:4). The oppressed do not resort to violence; instead they place their confidence in God's judgment at the end of time. (5:5-6). This passage brings the body of James's letter to an end.

5:7-11 Call to patient endurance

In concluding the letter (5:7-20), James does not use the customary method of ending letters. Instead, he uses other approaches also evident in Hellenistic letters. In this passage the theme of eschatology is taken up. Many New Testament letters contain eschatological references in their conclusions (see 1 Cor 16:22; 2 Pet 3:12-14; and Jude 18-21).

At the same time James connects back to themes that appeared explicitly in the introductory section, namely, steadfastness and endurance during trial (1:2-4 and 1:12-18). He urges the readers to have patient endurance until "the coming of the Lord" (5:7). This reference speaks of an imminent expectation for Jesus' coming at the end of time: "Behold, the Judge is standing before the gates" (5:9). This would indicate an early date for the writing. James helps his readers to see themselves as belonging to that long line of witnesses, the prophets, who remained ever faithful and persevered in their allegiance to the Lord (5:10). They are a prophetic community with values different from those of the world.

A second example of faithful perseverance is offered, namely, that of Job (5:11). James shows a reliance on the way the traditions about Job had developed in the intertestamental period, that is, the period of two centuries between the composition of the last book of the Old Testament and the first book of the New Testament. In the biblical book bearing his name, Job is hardly a patient person. However, in the intertestamental period (see the *Testament of Job* 1:5; 4:6; 27:6-7) he is presented this way. James uses this popular image of Job to challenge his hearers/readers to a life of patience and perseverance when faced with their own suffering and trials.

perseverance of Job, and you have seen the purpose of the Lord, because "the Lord is compassionate and merciful."

◄ [12]But above all, my brothers, do not swear, either by heaven or by earth or with any other oath, but let your "Yes" mean "Yes" and your "No" mean "No," that you may not incur condemnation.

IV. The Power of Prayer

Anointing of the Sick. [13]Is anyone among you suffering? He should pray.

Is anyone in good spirits? He should sing praise. [14]Is anyone among you ► sick? He should summon the presbyters of the church, and they should pray over him and anoint [him] with oil in the name of the Lord, [15]and the prayer ► of faith will save the sick person, and the Lord will raise him up. If he has committed any sins, he will be forgiven.

Confession and Intercession. [16]Therefore, confess your sins to one an- ► other and pray for one another, that

---

5:12 Call to avoid taking oaths

In this single verse James condemns the taking of oaths and appeals once again to his readers to examine their speech (see 1:26; 3:5-12; 4:11-12). In the Christian community one's word should be one's bond. There should be no need for taking oaths, since one should be able to presume truthfulness. The words "either by heaven or by earth" are substitutes for the original form of the oath and are used intentionally to avoid the validity of the oath, and hence its binding force. Jesus in the Sermon on the Mount speaks similarly about avoiding the taking of oaths (Matt 5:33-37).

5:13-18 Prayer

This concentration on the theme of prayer forms a fitting end to the letter, creating an "inclusion" with the opening, that is, the repetition, at the end of a section, of a word or phrase used at its beginning—in this case, prayer. In 1:5 James spoke about asking God for wisdom; now he argues that the way to obtain wisdom is through prayer. Not only is prayer the major theme of this section, but the various words for prayer are the controlling structural elements in its development. In every situation and need the appropriate response is that of prayer. In both suffering and joy people should raise their voices to God in prayer (5:13). The response of the sick is to call in the presbyters (or elders) of the church (5:14-15), who will pray over them and anoint them with oil in the name of the Lord.

James must be reflecting here some ritual in use in his community. Anointing with oil reminds the hearer/reader of the disciples' anointing the sick and casting out demons with the use of oil (Mark 6:13). When ill, one turns to God and asks the support of the community in praying to God for healing. The power of prayer cannot be measured.

you may be healed. The fervent prayer of a righteous person is very powerful. [17]Elijah was a human being like us; yet he prayed earnestly that it might not rain, and for three years and six months it did not rain upon the land. [18]Then he prayed again, and the sky gave rain and the earth produced its fruit.

Conversion of Sinners. [19]My brothers, if anyone among you should stray from the truth and someone bring him back, [20]he should know that whoever brings back a sinner from the error of his way will save his soul from death and will cover a multitude of sins.

Finally, Elijah, the prophet, is portrayed as a man of prayer. The effectiveness of Elijah is not related to any superhuman gifts or qualities he possessed, but to the fact that he prayed with great intensity and sincerity (5:17-18).

5:19-20 The great commission

The letter concludes somewhat abruptly with an admonition to bring back those who err from the error of their ways. 1 John 5:16 and Jude 22-23 also call on the community to pray that those who sin will change their ways. These three writings (James, 1 John, and Jude) bear witness to the existence of other ways of concluding ancient letters. Once again the community dimension of the letter shines through. Every member of the community shares a responsibility for one another. The commission with which James entrusts his hearers/readers is one that is confined to his own community. James wishes to ensure that those who belong to his community continue to remain true to their commitment. The call to conversion brings together everything that has been said throughout the letter. The hearers/readers are to take the author's instructions and put them into practice. The letter ends on a high note of confidence and assurance in the work of God's salvation.

The First Letter of Peter

Author

The writer identifies himself as "Peter, an apostle of Jesus Christ" (1:1). He also says that he was a witness to Christ's sufferings (5:1) and shares "in the glory to be revealed" (5:1). Although he addresses fellow elders (literally "presbyters"; 5:1), he speaks with authority, showing that he holds a position in the early Christian church that makes his voice respected.

At first glance the identification of the author with Peter, leader of the Twelve and witness to Christ's sufferings, seems justified. His position of authority within the early Christian community, his knowledge and use of the Old Testament, his association with both Silvanus and Mark as well as with the city of Rome—all these agree with what is known about Peter.

However, two major difficulties call this identification into question: *(a) the outstanding quality of the Greek* makes it among the best in the New Testament; *(b) the letter's theology bears a resemblance to Paul's theological ideas,* for example, some typical Pauline phrases appear: *in Christ* (3:16; 5:10, 14); *to serve* (1:12; 4:10). Paul's underlying stress on the importance of Jesus' death and resurrection is also well reflected in the thought of First Peter.

The above arguments militate against the writing coming directly from Peter. As with the letter of James, the writer invokes Peter's authority to resolve issues that had arisen after the apostle's death (A.D. 64). The letter probably originated from a circle of Peter's disciples in Rome, using the help of Silvanus and Mark (5:12-13), who account for some themes that were at home in Paul's thought. The letter was probably written in the early seventies, shortly after the destruction of Jerusalem in A.D. 70. The reference to Rome in a symbolic way as "Babylon" (5:13) would be a veiled reference to the Roman destruction of the city of Jerusalem (just as Babylon some five centuries earlier had destroyed Jerusalem). The attitude toward the state that First Peter endorses is very similar to Paul's views as expressed in Romans 13:1-7: they both uphold the state's authority (see 1 Pet 2:13-17).

Hearers/readers

The first letter of Peter identifies the hearers/readers as "the chosen sojourners of the dispersion in Pontus, Galatia, Cappadocia, Asia, and Bithynia" (1:1). The letter uses the reference to the dispersion differently from the way it occurs in the letter of James, where it refers to the scattering of Jewish-Christians outside the land of Palestine. In First Peter the term is used metaphorically, referring to Gentile Christians, who, as God's own people (2:9), are scattered like strangers in this world. Their real homeland is not here but in heaven. The places mentioned (Pontus, Galatia, Cappadocia, Asia, and Bithynia) are names for Roman provinces situated in the northern, central, and western parts of Asia Minor north of the Taurus Mountains. This territory covered an area of some 128,000 square miles. The address (1:1) indicates that this letter was meant to be circulated throughout the provinces of this region. The sequence of names probably indicates the route along which this letter would be circulated.

Major themes

First Peter is a very pastoral letter. The writer aims at strengthening the faith of his hearers/readers. He begins by recalling the Christian hope and inheritance based upon Jesus' resurrection from the dead (1:3-7). Jesus' sufferings are presented as a model for the hearers/readers, who themselves are enduring hostilities and suffering. They can be certain that just as Jesus' sufferings led to glory, so will theirs (1:11). The letter uses some remarkable imagery to describe the dignity of Christian believers: they are true heirs of the inheritance of God's people, Israel: the community is "a living stone" (2:5); "a chosen race, a royal priesthood, a holy nation, a people of his [God's] own" (2:9). This vision of their identity helps them face the challenges of living in a hostile world. Drawing upon well-known household codes, the writer gives direction on how to lead faithful Christian lives within this context.

The First Letter of Peter

I. Address

◄ **1** **Greeting.** ¹Peter, an apostle of Jesus Christ, to the chosen sojourners of the dispersion in Pontus, Galatia, Cappadocia, Asia, and Bithynia, ²in the foreknowledge of God the Father, through sanctification by the Spirit, for obedience and sprinkling with the blood of Jesus Christ: may grace and peace be yours in abundance.

1:1-2 Greetings

The writer opens the letter using the traditional Greco-Roman formula for a letter that identifies the sender, mentions the recipients, and concludes with a form of greeting. Referring to himself as "Peter, an apostle of Jesus Christ," the writer identifies himself with the leader of the original apostles (Mark 3:16). While the apostle Peter is unlikely to have actually written this letter himself (see Introduction, p. 29), the writer invokes Peter's authority for this letter. It is in this sense that this commentary refers to the author as Peter.

The readers are identified as "the chosen sojourners of the dispersion." The "dispersion," or Diaspora, is a technical term referring to Jews living outside their homeland, Palestine. However, the implied readers are certainly not Jews, nor are they Jewish Christians; rather, they are Christians who have come from the Gentile world. As such, this designation should be understood metaphorically as referring to Gentile Christians, who are "sojourners" here on earth, exiles from their true homeland in heaven. The writer uses the term "dispersion" differently from its usage in James 1:1.

The location of the recipients is more specifically identified as "Pontus, Galatia, Cappadocia, Asia, and Bithynia," names of Roman provinces in Asia Minor. The concept of "sojourners" implies that the way of life of these followers of Jesus is different from that of the world around them.

► This symbol indicates a cross reference number in the *Catechism of the Catholic Church*. See page 76 for number citations.

II. The Gift and Call of God
in Baptism

Blessing. ³Blessed be the God and Father of our Lord Jesus Christ, who in his great mercy gave us a new birth to a living hope through the resurrection of Jesus Christ from the dead, ⁴to an inheritance that is imperishable, undefiled, and unfading, kept in heaven for you ⁵who by the power of God are safeguarded through faith, to a salvation that is ready to be revealed in the final time. ⁶In this you rejoice, although now for a little while you may have to suffer through various trials, ⁷so that the genuineness of your faith, more precious than gold that is perishable even though tested by fire, may prove to be

---

They are also called "chosen sojourners," indicating that their identity comes from God's choice of them to become part of God's people. The writer refers to this same concept later when he identifies them as "a chosen race, a royal priesthood, a holy nation, a people of his own" (2:9), using the words of the Exodus covenant (see Exod 19:6).

Finally, the writer mentions the role of the Father, the Spirit, and Jesus Christ in the work of salvation. In doing so, he shows the basis for their identity as God's chosen ones: their choice is founded upon the Father's "foreknowledge" (1:2), particularly the Father's will and intention, to make them into his new people. God's choice of them also involves their "sanctification by the Spirit" (1:2), whose power enables them to lead their lives according to their new dignity. God's choice also includes their "sprinkling with the blood of Jesus Christ" (1:2). Just as Moses ratified the covenant of Sinai with the blood that he sprinkled on the altar (symbolizing God) and the people (Exod 24:3-8), now the new covenant is ratified with Jesus' blood that is sprinkled upon these hearers/readers. This phrase also prepares the reader for one of the major themes that runs throughout this letter, namely, the redemptive work of Jesus and its significance for believers (see 1:18-21; 2:21, 24; 3:18; 4:1, 11). The writer concludes with a prayer that grace and peace be multiplied among the hearers/readers.

1:3-12 Praise for salvation given by the Father, through the Son, and by the Spirit

In place of the traditional thanksgiving section found in Paul's letters, the writer immediately moves to the body of the letter. In the first part of the body the author reflects on the theme of the believer's identity (1:3-2:10). He begins by praising God the Father for the great gift of salvation. This blessing bears notable similarities to the opening of the letter to the Ephesians: "Blessed be the God and Father of our Lord Jesus Christ, who has blessed us in Christ with every spiritual blessing in the heavens" (Eph 1:3). The

A winding street in a village huddled against the strange rock formations of Cappadocia in Turkey

for praise, glory, and honor at the revelation of Jesus Christ. ⁸Although you have not seen him you love him; even though you do not see him now yet believe in him, you rejoice with an indescribable and glorious joy, ⁹as you attain the goal of [your] faith, the salvation of your souls.

◄ ¹⁰Concerning this salvation, prophets who prophesied about the grace that was to be yours searched and investigated it, ¹¹investigating the time and circumstances that the Spirit of Christ within them indicated when it testified in advance to the sufferings destined for Christ and the glories to follow them. ¹²It was revealed to them that they were serving not themselves but you with regard to the things that have now been announced to you by those who preached the good news to you [through] the holy Spirit sent from heaven, things into which angels longed to look.

Obedience. ¹³Therefore, gird up the loins of your mind, live soberly, and set

hearers/readers are reminded that they have been born to a new life through Jesus' resurrection (1 Pet 1:3).

This metaphor of new birth (1:3) has led some commentators to see this as a reference to baptism and to postulate that this writing was based upon an original baptismal homily. While this reads too much into the metaphor, the theology of baptism certainly influences this writer's thought. This new birth gives rise to the hope in an imperishable inheritance in heaven (1:3-5), and for this God is protecting them (1:5). The future hope is contrasted with their present experiences of suffering (1:6), which reveals the genuineness of their faith (1:7). Like precious gold that is purified by fire, so their new faith experiences testing or purification in order to prepare them for the coming of Jesus Christ (1:7).

The writer reminds the hearers/readers, who have not seen Jesus, how they love him and believe in him (1:8). Long ago the prophets of the Hebrew Scriptures foretold this salvation for which the believers are now hoping (1:10). These prophets were led by the Spirit to announce the message of the sufferings of Christ and his subsequent glory (1:11). The prophets show that the path from suffering to glory is the center of Jesus' saving work and the heart of the Christian way of life. This message clearly speaks to Peter's present readers, who are experiencing sufferings and trials. It reminds them that their rebirth in faith is more precious than gold, that it was foretold in the past and looks forward to a future glory.

1:13–2:3 Call to lead a holy life

The hearers/readers need also to respond to the new life they have received through a life that is worthy of their faith (1:13-14). Holiness should dominate their lives. The imagery of the Passover seems to lie be-

your hopes completely on the grace to be brought to you at the revelation of Jesus Christ. ¹⁴Like obedient children, do not act in compliance with the desires of your former ignorance ¹⁵but, as he who called you is holy, be holy yourselves in every aspect of your conduct, ¹⁶for it is written, "Be holy because I [am] holy."

Reverence. ¹⁷Now if you invoke as Father him who judges impartially according to each one's works, conduct yourselves with reverence during the time of your sojourning, ¹⁸realizing that you were ransomed from your futile conduct, handed on by your ancestors, not with perishable things like silver or gold ¹⁹but with the precious blood of Christ as of a spotless unblemished lamb. ²⁰He was known before the foundation of the world but revealed in the final time for you, ²¹who through him believe in God who raised him from the dead and gave him glory, so that your faith and hope are in God.

Mutual Love. ²²Since you have purified yourselves by obedience to the truth for sincere mutual love, love one another intensely from a [pure] heart. ²³You have been born anew, not from perishable but from imperishable seed, through the living and abiding word of God, ²⁴for:

> "All flesh is like grass,
>> and all its glory like the flower
>>> of the field;
> the grass withers,
>> and the flower wilts;
> ²⁵but the word of the Lord remains
>> forever."

This is the word that has been proclaimed to you.

2 **God's House and People.** ¹Rid yourselves of all malice and all deceit, insincerity, envy, and all slander; ²like newborn infants, long for pure spiritual milk so that through it you may grow into salvation, ³for you have tasted that the Lord is good. ⁴Come to him, a living stone, rejected by human beings but chosen and precious in the sight of God, ⁵and, like living stones, let yourselves be built into a spiritual house to be a holy priesthood to offer

---

hind this section. At Sinai, the LORD God was identified as the Holy One, who called on the Israelites to be holy: "For I, the LORD, am your God; and you shall make and keep yourselves holy, because I am holy" (Lev 11:44; 19:2). First Peter quotes this text and addresses the same call to holiness to his hearers/readers: they are to imitate God in all their actions (1:16). To be holy means to be different, to be set apart. The Israelites were a nation set apart for the worship of God alone. The same is true of Christians: they are called to be different in that their way of life sets them apart from the nations around them (as the writer indicated in the opening of the letter when he referred to them as "sojourners" [1:1]). Their values do not come from the world, but have God as their source. Their new life of holiness enables them to address God as "Father," which inspires an attitude of "reverence" (1:17) for the mystery of God's love and rule over all.

spiritual sacrifices acceptable to God through Jesus Christ. ⁶For it says in scripture:

"Behold, I am laying a stone in Zion,
a cornerstone, chosen and precious,
and whoever believes in it shall not be put to shame."

⁷Therefore, its value is for you who have faith, but for those without faith:

"The stone which the builders rejected
has become the cornerstone,"

⁸and

"A stone that will make people stumble,

The author goes on to remind the hearers/readers of certain truths they have accepted. Continuing with the Passover theme, he reminds them that just as the Israelites were ransomed from slavery, so have they been ransomed "with the precious blood of Christ" (1:19), not with precious metals "like silver or gold" (1:18). They have been ransomed from the futile way of life they inherited from their pagan ancestors (1:18). First Peter compares the work of Jesus to that of "a spotless unblemished lamb" (1:19): they have received their redemption through the blood of the spotless lamb (Isa 53:7-10). This is a further reminder of the Passover motif (Exod 12:1-30). Through his death, Jesus has ransomed Christians, enabling them to place their trust, their faith, and their hope in God (1:21).

The author repeats many of the themes introduced at the beginning of the letter (1:22–2:3). They are called to "love one another intensely" (1:22). This love is a response to Christ's work, which planted "the imperishable seed" in them (1:23). In support, the author quotes Isaiah 40:6-8, which contrasts the frailty and transitory nature of human life and its accomplishments with the word of the Lord, which remains forever (1:24-25). Their faith endures forever because God is trustworthy. Their growth in new life involves two dimensions: first of all, the stripping away of all vices (2:1) hindering that growth, and the nourishment and enjoyment of the new life they have received (2:2-3). The author concludes with an allusion to Psalm 34:9: "Taste and see how good the LORD is; / happy the man who takes refuge in him."

2:4-10 A holy people

Two metaphors dominate this passage: that of a living stone (2:4-8) and that of a people (2:9-10). The author uses numerous texts from the Hebrew Scriptures to illustrate his vision. The image of a living stone is applied to his hearers/readers. While humanity has rejected them, God has specially chosen them as "living stones" (2:5). They should allow God to build them into a spiritual household to become a holy priesthood able to offer accept-

and a rock that will make them
fall."
They stumble by disobeying the word,
as is their destiny.
   ⁹But you are "a chosen race, a royal
priesthood, a holy nation, a people of
his own, so that you may announce the
praises" of him who called you out of
darkness into his wonderful light.
   ¹⁰Once you were "no people"
      but now you are God's people;

you "had not received mercy"
   but now you have received
      mercy.

III. The Christian in
a Hostile World

Christian Examples. ¹¹Beloved, I
urge you as aliens and sojourners to
keep away from worldly desires that
wage war against the soul. ¹²Maintain

---

able sacrifices to God through Jesus Christ (2:4-5) who is a "living stone"
(2:4).

Three quotations from the Hebrew Scriptures illustrate the meaning.
Christ is the "cornerstone" or foundation stone (see Isa 28:16), and whoever
places trust in him will be supported (2:6). Further, this living stone (which
is Christ) was rejected (2:7) but has become the cornerstone (see Ps 118:22).
Finally, he uses Isaiah 8:14 very freely to indicate how Jesus becomes an ob-
stacle and a stumbling block for some (2:8). This metaphor of the living
stone and its supportive Hebrew Scripture texts illustrates two things: it
shows, first of all, how Jesus Christ is the model for the believing community: just like Jesus, believers are chosen by God but rejected by humanity,
especially the world of the pagans. Secondly, since Christ is the cornerstone
and foundation for faith, believers are being built in him into a spiritual
house as a holy priesthood offering true spiritual worship to God (2:5).

The second metaphor of a holy people (2:9-10) expressing the true
identity of Christian believers is revealed in four phrases: a chosen race, a
royal priesthood, a holy nation, God's own people. These phrases are all
derived from Exodus 19:5-6. Christians as God's possession give worship
to God through the power of Jesus' death and resurrection. Their most important characteristic is that they have become "God's people," just as Israel of old was chosen as God's people (2:10). Reflecting on Hosea 1:6-9
and 2:25, the writer proclaims that the readers were originally separated
far from God, but now they have been brought into God's household to
become God's people (2:10).

2:11-12 Conduct in a pagan environment
The author now begins a second major theme of the letter, namely, the
Christian life of witness in the context of a Gentile world (2:11–4:11). The
readers are to consider themselves as "aliens and sojourners" in this present

good conduct among the Gentiles, so that if they speak of you as evildoers, they may observe your good works and glorify God on the day of visitation.

Christian Citizens. ¹³Be subject to every human institution for the Lord's sake, whether it be to the king as supreme ¹⁴or to governors as sent by him for the punishment of evildoers and the approval of those who do good. ¹⁵For it is the will of God that by doing good you may silence the ignorance of foolish people. ¹⁶Be free, yet ▶ without using freedom as a pretext for evil, but as slaves of God. ¹⁷Give honor to all, love the community, fear God, honor the king.

Christian Slaves. ¹⁸Slaves, be subject to your masters with all reverence, not only to those who are good and eq-

world (2:11). Since their true homeland is to be found in heaven (1:1), they are to conduct themselves in this world as though they are just passing through. Their way of life should bear witness to their beliefs among Gentiles (2:12). Even though Gentiles abuse them, Christians are called to respond in a manner worthy of their beliefs. This witness should bring the Gentiles to revise their view of Christians and ultimately to confess and praise their God at the end of time.

2:13-17 Respect for civil authorities

This passage considers the principles outlined above (2:11-12), which called believers to lead lives as "aliens and sojourners" in this world. This is not a call for believers to become a withdrawal sect such as the Qumran community; rather, Christians are called upon to honor civil authorities. Belief in the Lord Jesus should lead Christians to accept the authority of the emperor and governors, acknowledging their right to punish wrongdoers and to reward those who act for good (2:13-14). This witness should silence those who are suspicious of Christians (2:15; see 2:12). The best answer to those hostile to the Christian community is the life-witness of obedient Christians (2:15). Baptism has set believers free from the stipulations of the Jewish Torah (as Paul indicates forcefully in Gal 3:23-27), as well as from slavery to the elemental powers of the world (in the context of a pagan world [Col 2:20-23]). This freedom is not a freedom for license, but a freedom to lead one's life under God's rule (2:16).

The first letter of Peter upholds a positive relationship between Christians and the state; Christians are urged to acknowledge and to give honor to all: the community, God, and the emperor as supreme ruler (2:17). The letter gives expression to a consciousness of the Christian's double obligation of fulfilling God's will as well as the demands of political authority. It is the same issue addressed in the saying of Jesus: "Repay

uitable but also to those who are perverse. [19]For whenever anyone bears the pain of unjust suffering because of consciousness of God, that is a grace. [20]But what credit is there if you are patient when beaten for doing wrong? But if you are patient when you suffer for doing what is good, this is a grace before God. [21]For to this you have been called, because Christ also suffered for you, leaving you an example that you should follow in his footsteps.

[22]"He committed no sin,
and no deceit was found in his
mouth."

[23]When he was insulted, he returned no insult; when he suffered, he did not threaten; instead, he handed himself over to the one who judges justly. [24]He himself bore our sins in his body upon

to Caesar what belongs to Caesar and to God what belongs to God" (Mark 12:17). Clearly, First Peter reflects a situation very different from that of the book of Revelation, where Christians are being persecuted by the state for not participating in emperor worship, a context that First Peter does not envisage here. The thoughts of First Peter are very similar to those found in Romans 13:1-7, which may indicate evidence of a common tradition that both First Peter and Paul are using independently.

2:18–3:7 Household instructions

First Peter uses the literary form of "household codes" to express his instructions. A number of such codes or lists appear in the New Testament letters (for example, Col 3:18–4:1; Eph 5:21–6:9; 1 Tim 2:8-15; 5:1-2; 6:1-2; and here 1 Pet 2:18–3:7). These lists describe the ethical obligations members of a household have toward one another. Such lists embrace every possible relationship within society and were very popular among the philosophers of that time.

The developing Christian communities drew up similar ethical lists depicting the way their members should interact with one another as well as with every level of society. The need for such directions was felt most urgently in largely Gentile Christian communities. They wanted to witness to their faith in Jesus Christ in such a way that the wider society would see their faith influencing them to become valuable citizens within society. These lists are an illustration of how the Lordship of Jesus Christ transforms the lives of believers to affect every relationship and to attract others to make a similar confession in the Lord Jesus Christ. In this household list First Peter gives attention to the relationships of slaves, wives, and husbands. When interpreting these household codes, they must be read in the context of their own world and not simply transposed into a twenty-first-century society that would describe these relationships very differently.

39

the cross, so that, free from sin, we might live for righteousness. By his wounds you have been healed. ²⁵For you had gone astray like sheep, but you have now returned to the shepherd and guardian of your souls.

3 **Christian Spouses.** ¹Likewise, you wives should be subordinate to your husbands so that, even if some disobey the word, they may be won over without a word by their wives' conduct ²when they observe your reverent and chaste behavior. ³Your adornment should not be an external one: braiding the hair, wearing gold jewelry, or dressing in fine clothes, ⁴but rather the hidden character of the heart, expressed in the imperishable beauty of a gentle and calm disposition, which is precious in the sight of God. ⁵For this is also how the holy women who hoped in God once used to adorn themselves and were subordinate to their husbands; ⁶thus Sarah obeyed Abraham, calling him "lord."

2:18-25 Attitude of slaves toward their masters

According to First Peter, belief in God should lead slaves to accept their masters' authority and to endure suffering even when innocent (2:18-19). First Peter differs from the traditional advice to slaves by focusing on the difficult lot of slaves and by considering situations where they suffer unjustly. They are invited to view their unjust sufferings in the light of the unjust suffering of Christ. In such situations, they are called to unite with the sufferings of Christ by following the example that he set. The description of the suffering and death of Christ on our behalf (2:22-24) is presented in terms of the Suffering Servant of Isaiah 52:13–53:12. Christian slaves are called upon to live out their commitment to Christ in a concrete way by imitating his suffering. Christ obtained salvation through suffering for sinners, so Christian slaves can bring others to salvation through the witness of their sufferings. No mention is made here of the responsibilities of masters toward their slaves!

3:1-7 Attitude of wives and husbands

First Peter continues the household code with reference to wives and husbands. Again its thoughts are rooted in the social structure and attitudes of the first century A.D. Christian wives are instructed on how to relate to their husbands who are not believers (3:1). By the witness of their lives and through their belief in Christ, they hope ultimately to win over their husbands to the Christian faith (3:1-2). The wives' concern should not focus on extravagant externals, such as "braiding the hair, gold jewelry, or dressing in fine clothes" (3:3); instead, they should cultivate a gentle internal disposition at peace with God and one another (3:4). Reaching back into the tradition of the Hebrew Scriptures, First Peter holds up Sarah for imitation because of the way in which she respected Abraham by calling

You are her children when you do what is good and fear no intimidation.

⁷Likewise, you husbands should live with your wives in understanding, showing honor to the weaker female sex, since we are joint heirs of the gift of life, so that your prayers may not be hindered.

Christian Conduct.⁸Finally, all of you, be of one mind, sympathetic, loving toward one another, compassionate, humble. ⁹Do not return evil for evil, or insult for insult; but, on the contrary, a blessing, because to this you were called, that you might inherit a blessing. ¹⁰For:

"Whoever would love life
    and see good days
must keep the tongue from evil
    and the lips from speaking deceit,
¹¹must turn from evil and do good,
    seek peace and follow after it.

him "lord" or "master" (3:6; see Gen 18:12 LXX), a term that indicates respect and honor for the husband. Likewise the wives of pagan husbands should demonstrate respect and honor for their husbands, showing that they are daughters of Sarah (3:6). Abraham and Sarah were important figures in the world of early Christianity (Rom 4:19-25; 9:9; Gal 4:22-31).

Husbands are also instructed to examine their relationship with their wives (3:7). While the cultural view of women dominates this picture ("showing honor to the weaker female sex"), yet the equality of women with men is acknowledged, since in the life of Christ "we are joint heirs of the gift of life" (3:7; see also Gal 3:28: "There is neither Jew nor Greek, there is neither slave nor free person, there is not male and female; for you are all one in Christ Jesus"). First Peter shows that proper relationships cannot be separated from a relationship with God that is expressed in prayer (3:7).

3:8-12 General advice to the whole community

This section brings the household instructions to an end. Generally, household codes would turn to consider the relationship of parents and children at this point. Instead, First Peter turns attention to relationships within the entire community and urges unity and love for one another so that their way of life will truly reflect a Christian community (3:8). Instead of returning evil for evil, they are called to react with a blessing (3:9). That is the way Jesus acted, and they are called to act in like manner (see 2:21-25). Their unity with Christ gives direction to the way they lead their lives. First Peter quotes Psalm 34:13-17 to remind the community that "whoever would love life . . . must turn from evil and do good" (3:10-11).

3:13-17 Christian attitude toward suffering

The Christian is exhorted to have confidence in the midst of suffering. The sufferings envisaged here do not necessarily point to some state

¹²For the eyes of the Lord are on the
righteous
and his ears turned to their
prayer,
but the face of the Lord is against
evildoers."

Christian Suffering. ¹³Now who is
going to harm you if you are enthusias-
tic for what is good? ¹⁴But even if you
should suffer because of righteousness,
blessed are you. Do not be afraid or ter-
rified with fear of them, ¹⁵but sanctify
Christ as Lord in your hearts. Always
be ready to give an explanation to anyone who asks you for a reason for your
hope, ¹⁶but do it with gentleness and
reverence, keeping your conscience
clear, so that, when you are maligned,
those who defame your good conduct
in Christ may themselves be put to

persecution, as was the case with the book of Revelation. It seems that
Gentiles living in the same society with Christians cannot understand
their lifestyle and values. The Gentiles respond with abuse and ridicule,
and ostracize them because of their commitment to the Lord Jesus, but
this should not cause them to be afraid (3:14). When challenged, Christians should be ready to witness to their faith (3:15). First Peter calls on
Christians to make their defense in gentleness and with respect, while
being willing to accept suffering, if that is God's will (3:16-17).

3:18-22 Example of Christ

Jesus suffered as an innocent person for the guilty. His death is the reason the hearers/readers and indeed all Christians are now able to ap-
proach God (3:18). His suffering led to the ultimate experience of death.
But death was not the end. He "was brought to life in the spirit" (3:18) and
went "to preach to the spirits in prison" (3:19). It is not too clear who these
spirits were. Possibly First Peter has in mind an interpretation of Genesis
6:1-4, where evil angels were held responsible for leading humanity
astray into an ever greater wickedness that ultimately provoked God's
righteous judgment in sending the flood. These evil angels were impris-
oned in a pit after their sin with women. Jesus' proclamation to them by
his death and resurrection is a way of demonstrating his victory over the
forces of evil: these evil spirits no longer have power over humanity.

This example of Christ's suffering and consequent triumph in the resurrection gives hope to Christians who innocently endure suffering and
persecution. Because Christ's triumph over evil is complete, Christians
have nothing to fear. Christ has redeemed them from the powers of evil
and death and has given them future hope through their new birth in
Christ. Reference to Noah (3:20) is also significant. First Peter argues that
just as God rescued the faithful Noah from the evil world by means of
water, so too God liberates faithful Christians from the evils of their world

shame. [17]For it is better to suffer for doing good, if that be the will of God, than for doing evil.

[18]For Christ also suffered for sins once, the righteous for the sake of the unrighteous, that he might lead you to God. Put to death in the flesh, he was brought to life in the spirit. [19]In it he also went to preach to the spirits in prison, [20]who had once been disobedient while God patiently waited in the days of Noah during the building of the ark, in which a few persons, eight in all, were saved through water. [21]This prefigured baptism, which saves you now. It is not a removal of dirt from the body but an appeal to God for a clear conscience, through the resurrection of Jesus Christ, [22]who has gone into heaven and is at the right hand of God, with angels, authorities, and powers subject to him.

4 **Christian Restraint.** [1]Therefore, since Christ suffered in the flesh, arm yourselves also with the same attitude (for whoever suffers in the flesh

---

by means of the waters of baptism (3:21). Jesus' resurrection makes the waters of baptism effective and brings salvation to those who accept it (3:21). Through his resurrection, Jesus Christ shares God's power, and all authority in the universe is subjected to him (3:22). Behind this beautiful description of the saving work of Christ lies a creedal formula in use in the early church. Not only does First Peter use the Hebrew Scriptures as a source to support his teaching, he also uses the language of the liturgy that permeates the Christian community:

> Put to death in the flesh, brought to life in the spirit, he went to preach to the spirits in prison, and having gone into heaven, he is at the right hand of God, making angels, authorities and powers subject to him (3:18, 19, 22; see also 1 Tim 3:16).

This passage has enormous importance for Christian believers. Just as Christ's death brings life, so too Christian suffering is considered life-generating. Christians participate in Christ's death and resurrection through baptism. As Christ "was put to death in the flesh" and "was brought to life in the spirit" (3:18), so Christians die to their sins and are made alive in the spirit through baptism. Christian believers are made aware that they share both in Christ's sufferings and in his resurrection.

4:1-6 Christians live according to God's will

First Peter connects back to the previous section by stressing that Christians who lead a life of suffering with Christ are also dedicated to avoiding a life of sin (4:1) and living according to God's will (4:2). Their lifestyle distances them from the way of life of their Gentile neighbors. First Peter presents a list of vices (4:3) similar to the lists that Paul used in his letters (see Rom 1:29-31; 1 Tim 1:9-10; 2 Tim 3:2-5). The vices described

has broken with sin), ²so as not to spend what remains of one's life in the flesh on human desires, but on the will of God. ³For the time that has passed is sufficient for doing what the Gentiles like to do: living in debauchery, evil desires, drunkenness, orgies, carousing, and wanton idolatry. ⁴They are surprised that you do not plunge into the same swamp of profligacy, and they vilify you; ⁵but they will give an account to him who stands ready to judge the living and the dead. ⁶For this is why the ▶ gospel was preached even to the dead that, though condemned in the flesh in human estimation, they might live in the spirit in the estimation of God.

Christian Charity. ⁷The end of all ▶ things is at hand. Therefore, be serious and sober for prayers. ⁸Above all, let ▶

---

here reflect the type of feasts that pagans used to celebrate. Before becoming Christians, First Peter's hearers/readers used to participate in these celebrations, but now, having embraced Christ and become God's people, they distance themselves from such activities (4:4).

Further, First Peter envisages a preaching of the good news to those who have died (4:6). While Peter does not mention who does the preaching, it seems that he has 3:18-20 in mind, where Jesus preaches after his death. This time, however, the preaching is not to the powers of evil but to those who have died. While the exact reference of "the dead" is disputed, the best explanation is that "the dead" are Christians who had heard and accepted the gospel message but subsequently died before Christ's return.

For early Christians this was an enormous problem, since many believed that Christ would return during their own lifetime. Here First Peter assures his hearers/believers that while in the eyes of the world these Christians have ended up in death in the same way as those who have not believed ("condemned in the flesh in human estimation"), they now share in Christ's triumph over death through resurrection ("they might live in the spirit in the estimation of God," 4:6). First Peter assures his hearers/readers that as Christ triumphed over the powers of evil (3:18-22), so those who believed in him and his message would share with him in that triumph in the resurrection.

4:7-11 Living with the expectation of the end time

With this passage the author brings to an end the second major theme of the letter, namely, the Christian life of witness in the context of a Gentile world (2:11-4:11). First Peter reminds the hearers/readers that the eschatological hour is near (4:7). Consequently, the community must lead its life marked by prayer (4:7), love (4:8), hospitality (4:9), and service of one another (4:10). First Peter presents love as the central virtue "because love covers a multitude of sins" (4:8). This maxim appears in the Hebrew

your love for one another be intense, because love covers a multitude of sins. ⁹Be hospitable to one another without complaining. ¹⁰As each one has received a gift, use it to serve one another as good stewards of God's varied grace. ¹¹Whoever preaches, let it be with the words of God; whoever serves, let it be with the strength that God supplies, so that in all things God may be glorified through Jesus Christ, to whom belong glory and dominion forever and ever. Amen.

IV. Advice to the Persecuted

Trial of Persecution. ¹²Beloved, do not be surprised that a trial by fire is occurring among you, as if something strange were happening to you. ¹³But rejoice to the extent that you share in the sufferings of Christ, so that when his glory is revealed you may also rejoice exultantly. ¹⁴If you are insulted for the name of Christ, blessed are you, for the Spirit of glory and of God rests upon you. ¹⁵But let no one among you

---

Scriptures (Prov 10:12; Ps 32:1), as well as elsewhere in the New Testament (Jas 5:20) and in early Christian literature (*1 Clem* 50:5).

First Peter's quotation of Proverbs 10:12 is closer to the Hebrew text, although he usually quotes from the Greek translation (LXX). This could indicate that he is relying upon the way in which it was being quoted in early Christian tradition. While the exact meaning of this proverb is somewhat vague, the general intent is clear: in loving others one fulfills the essence of the gospel call to love God and neighbor. Consequently, one experiences God's forgiveness for all sins. This passage culminates in a doxology to the praise of God (4:11).

4:12-19 Suffering as a Christian

The writer begins the third and final section of the letter (4:12–5:11) taking up themes that were introduced elsewhere in the letter. All the themes bear a strong eschatological emphasis. First Peter 4:12 returns to the theme of suffering that has dominated the letter. The readers are invited to see their sufferings as a purification (4:12) and as a sharing in Christ's sufferings (4:13). That should be cause for rejoicing, because those who have suffered are promised that they will share in Christ's glory (4:14). The present sufferings initiate the eschatological judgment within God's household (4:17). The prospect of suffering should not cause fear among Christians; rather, it should be seen to be "in accord with God's will" (4:19), and consequently they should place themselves in the care of their ever "faithful creator" (4:19).

5:1-5 Exhortation to the leaders of the community

The author identifies himself as a "fellow presbyter and witness to the sufferings of Christ" (5:1). The term "presbyter" or "elder" reflects the Jew-

be made to suffer as a murderer, a thief, an evildoer, or as an intriguer. ¹⁶But whoever is made to suffer as a Christian should not be ashamed but glorify God because of the name. ¹⁷For it is time for the judgment to begin with the household of God; if it begins with us, how will it end for those who fail to obey the gospel of God?

¹⁸"And if the righteous one is barely saved,
where will the godless and the sinner appear?"

¹⁹As a result, those who suffer in accord with God's will hand their souls over to a faithful creator as they do good.

Advice to Presbyters. ¹So I exhort the presbyters among you, as a fellow presbyter and witness to the sufferings of Christ and one who has a share in the glory to be revealed. ²Tend the flock of God in your midst, [overseeing] not by constraint but willingly, as God would have it, not for shameful profit but eagerly. ³Do not lord it over those assigned to you, but be examples to the flock. ⁴And when the chief Shepherd is revealed, you will receive the unfading crown of glory.

Advice to the Community. ⁵Likewise, you younger members, be subject to the presbyters. And all of you, clothe

---

ish world, where the leaders of the community were identified by this term. It referred not simply to age but rather to the role exercised by leaders within a community. As such, First Peter exhorts his fellow elders (or leaders) to take care of the community that has been entrusted to them (5:1-2).

In offering advice to the elders, the writer uses traditional imagery. Earlier in the letter First Peter had referred to Christ as the "shepherd and guardian of your souls" (2:25). Now the leaders of the community are called to care for "the flock of God" that has been entrusted to them (5:2). First Peter defines the type of leadership they should exercise through a number of contrasts: they should carry out their leadership role "willingly" (not "by constraint") (5:2). They should not be inspired by greed, but by a desire for service (5:2). Finally, they should "not lord it over" those in their care, but should be examples to the community ("the flock," 5:3). Finally, First Peter uses the image of Christ the shepherd to encourage them to act like shepherds toward those entrusted to their care (4:4). This brings the author to address a universal appeal to the members of the community: "God opposes the proud, but bestows favor on the humble" (4:5; see Prov 3:34).

5:6-11 Final exhortations: trust God

This section draws the body of the letter to a conclusion. The readers are called to humble themselves (5:6); to cast all their anxiety upon God (5:7), to keep alert (5:8). The devil, like a roaring lion (see Ps 22:14), is inciting the Gentiles to persecute the Christians. What First Peter's readers are experiencing is not unique, because Christians throughout the world

yourselves with humility in your dealings with one another, for:

"God opposes the proud
but bestows favor on the
humble."

⁶So humble yourselves under the mighty hand of God, that he may exalt you in due time. ⁷Cast all your worries upon him because he cares for you.

⁸Be sober and vigilant. Your opponent the devil is prowling around like a roaring lion looking for [someone] to devour. ⁹Resist him, steadfast in faith, knowing that your fellow believers throughout the world undergo the same sufferings. ¹⁰The God of all grace who called you to his eternal glory through Christ [Jesus] will himself restore, confirm, strengthen, and establish you after you have suffered a little. ¹¹To him be dominion forever. Amen

.

V. Conclusion

¹²I write you this briefly through Silvanus, whom I consider a faithful brother, exhorting you and testifying that this is the true grace of God. Remain firm in it. ¹³The chosen one at Babylon sends you greeting, as does Mark, my son. ¹⁴Greet one another with a loving kiss. Peace to all of you who are in Christ.

---

are enduring similar sufferings and persecutions (5:9). A doxology concludes the body of the letter. The author promises that Christ will support and strengthen them in this struggle (5:10-11).

5:12-14 Final greeting

The letter concludes in the traditional way with personal greetings. Silvanus is identified either as the bearer of the letter or the one who acted as Peter's scribe in writing it (5:12). Greetings are sent from "the chosen one at Babylon" (5:13), referring to the church in Rome (see Introduction, p. 29; the book of Revelation also refers to Rome as Babylon in 14:8; 17:5; 18:2). Greetings also comes from "Mark, my son," referring probably to John Mark from Jerusalem (Acts 12:12-17) and indicating that Peter was responsible for his conversion to the Christian faith ("my son," 5:13). The Christian greeting "Peace to all of you who are in Christ" concludes the letter.

The Letter of Jude

The letter of Jude, one of the shortest New Testament writings, is also one of the most intriguing. It was taken up almost in its entirety into Second Peter. Its place in the canon has often been challenged, not least of all by the early church, which was concerned with its usage of the apocryphal books of *1 Enoch* and the *Assumption of Moses*.

Author

The writer of the letter identifies himself as: "Jude, a slave of Jesus Christ and brother of James" (v. 1). In the New Testament world the name Jude (or more accurately "Judas") was quite common. Matthew 13:55 notes that James, "the brother of the Lord" and leader of the Jerusalem church, had a brother named Judas: "Is not his mother named Mary and his brothers James, Joseph, Simon, and Judas?" The writer, then, identifies himself with this James, the leader of the Jerusalem church and "brother of the Lord."

However, the information we glean about the author from the text presents some difficulties in making this identification: (a) *The writer's vocabulary shows a good knowledge of Greek*—some twenty-two words occur only in this letter in the New Testament (excluding Second Peter's borrowing from Jude). (b) *The opening greetings,* "May mercy, peace, and love be yours in abundance" (v. 2), differ from the common Pauline greetings: "Grace . . . and peace" (e.g., Phil 1:2). However there are similarities with the opening of a number of other New Testament letters. For example, a threefold listing of "grace, mercy, and peace" occurs in 1 Timothy 1:2; 2 Timothy 1:2; and 2 John 3. The letters of Peter have the greetings as "May grace and peace be yours in abundance." The opening of Polycarp's letter to the Philippians (written before A.D. 155) also has a similar form: "Mercy and peace from God Almighty and Jesus Christ our Savior be multiplied to you." All this shows that a variation of the form used by Jude was common in the postapostolic period. (c) *The writer comes from a period after the apostles:* In verses 17-18 the author does not include himself in the group of apostles but gives the impression that he belongs to a later generation.

All these arguments point to the letter coming from a second-generation Christian at the end of the first century. As with the letters of James and First Peter, the writer invokes the name of Jude because he wishes to endorse his authority in settling problems that have arisen in a certain area of the Christian church.

Hearers/readers

The letter is an immediate response to a sudden danger arising within certain Christian communities. Intruders entering the communities are undermining their traditional faith as well as their morals. It is addressed: "To those who are called, beloved in God the Father and kept safe for Jesus Christ" (v. 1). The writing does not provide a detailed description of the readers or of their opponents. From the letter some information can be deduced about the first hearers/readers of this letter. From its tone the letter seems to be directed to a definite church or group of churches. The use of the Hebrew Scriptures and apocryphal allusions indicate a Jewish-Christian community. The writer's identification of himself as "brother of James" must indicate a community in which James's authority was recognized. The cultural mixture of Jewish and Greek elements in this letter is similar to that of the letter of James and would perhaps argue for a similar destination. Given this information, the area of Syria or northern Palestine would seem to be the most likely destination.

Genre and main thoughts

While this writing commences with the traditional opening formula of a letter, it lacks final personal greetings and ends with a doxology praising God. A close reading reveals that the literary form of a letter suits it best. In verses 3-4 the writer shows his pastoral intent of writing to a group of Christians for whom he holds responsibility. He aims at helping them meet the new challenges arising from the inroads of intruding teachers within their community. Drawing upon their common heritage, the writer warns his hearers/readers about the dangers they face. It is a wonderful record of an early Christian church struggling to hold firm to the traditional faith, while at the same time opening up to the new culture around it.

The Letter of Jude

Address and Greeting. ¹Jude, a slave of Jesus Christ and brother of James, to those who are called, beloved in God the Father and kept safe for Jesus Christ: ²may mercy, peace, and love be yours in abundance.

Occasion for Writing. ³Beloved, although I was making every effort to write to you about our common salvation, I now feel a need to write to encourage you to contend for the faith that was once for all handed down to ▶

Verses 1-2 Greetings

Using the customary format of a letter, the writer refers to himself as Jude, "a slave of Jesus Christ" (see Jas 1:1; Titus 1:1). This phrase "slave of Jesus Christ" recalls the biblical tradition that identifies figures like Moses (1 Kgs 8:53) and David (1 Kgs 8:66) as a "slave of God." As with the letters of James and First Peter, the writer invokes the authority of an apostolic figure, Jude, for this letter (see Introduction, pp. 48–49). It is in this sense that this commentary refers to the author as Jude. Since he is less well known, he identifies himself further as the "brother of James" (probably James "the brother of the Lord," Gal 1:19). This would imply that he is writing to Jewish Christians, since James was an important figure in their world. The writer identifies the readers in a general sense as "those who are called." Paul refers to his hearers/readers in Rome in a similar way (Rom 1:6). Finally, he extends greetings: "may mercy, peace, and love be yours in abundance" (v. 2; see 1 Tim 1:2; 2 Tim 1:2).

Verses 3-4 Occasion for the letter

The usual thanksgiving section is missing. The author intended to write to his readers about their common salvation, but a more urgent topic arose. Many false teachers have entered the community of his hearers/readers

▶ This symbol indicates a cross reference number in the *Catechism of the Catholic Church*. See page 76 for number citations.

A modern road snaking through the upper Galilee Valley

the holy ones. ⁴For there have been some intruders, who long ago were designated for this condemnation, godless persons, who pervert the grace of our God into licentiousness and who deny our only Master and Lord, Jesus Christ.

⁵I wish to remind you, although you know all things, that [the] Lord who once saved a people from the land of Egypt later destroyed those who did not believe. ⁶The angels too, who did not keep to their own domain but deserted their proper dwelling, he has kept in eternal chains, in gloom, for the judgment of the great day. ⁷Likewise, Sodom, Gomorrah, and the surrounding towns, which, in the same manner as they, indulged in sexual promiscuity and practiced unnatural vice, serve as an example by undergoing a punishment of eternal fire.

⁸Similarly, these dreamers nevertheless also defile the flesh, scorn lordship, and revile glorious beings. ⁹Yet the

---

and are distorting their faith, especially their belief in Jesus Christ. The writer urges the hearers/readers "to contend for the faith" (v. 3). This image is taken from the world of athletic contests. Since only one person can win the prize, Jude exhorts his readers to be the ones who win in this struggle. He says two things about these intruders (v. 4): they "pervert the grace of our God into licentiousness," implying their moral degeneration into sexual immorality; and they "deny our only Master and Lord, Jesus Christ," implying doctrinal teaching that refuses to acknowledge the Lordship of Jesus and his teaching.

Verses 5-7 God punishes those who are unfaithful

The phrase "I wish to remind you" is a marker identifying the beginning of the argument based on past examples. Using three examples, Jude reminds his hearers/readers of figures who fell from positions of favor with God and were punished because of their sins.

His first reference is to God's chosen people, whom God liberated from slavery in Egypt. They complained against God in the desert and were destroyed because of their lack of faith (v. 5; see Num 14).

In the second example, angels of God came down to earth to seek out women (Gen 6:1-4). They were punished by God in chains and darkness until the judgment day (v. 6; see *1 Enoch* 10:4-6, 12-13).

Thirdly, Sodom and Gomorrah were punished in eternal fire because of their "sexual promiscuity" (v. 7).

Verses 8-9 Application

These verses consider the intruding teachers: they "defile the flesh" (like Sodom and Gomorrah, they practice sexual immorality); they "scorn lordship" (like the Israelites at the time of the Exodus, they reject God's

archangel Michael, when he argued with the devil in a dispute over the body of Moses, did not venture to pronounce a reviling judgment upon him but said, "May the Lord rebuke you!" ¹⁰But these people revile what they do not understand and are destroyed by what they know by nature like irrational animals. ¹¹Woe to them! They followed the way of Cain, abandoned themselves to Balaam's error for the sake of gain, and perished in the rebellion of Korah. ¹²These are blemishes on your love feasts, as they carouse fearlessly and look after themselves. They are waterless clouds blown about by

covenant and authority); and they "revile glorious beings" (like the angels, they refuse to serve and obey God). The implication is that these false teachers will experience similar judgments and punishments.

In verse 9 Jude cites a story taken from an apocryphal Jewish writing, *The Assumption of Moses* (though many modern scholars prefer to name it more correctly *The Testament of Moses*). This work exists in only one Latin manuscript text, dated from the sixth century A.D. Unfortunately this manuscript ends before the description of the death of Moses. The story that Jude narrates here is presumed to refer to the lost ending of this manuscript.

The book of Deuteronomy says that Moses died and was buried in the land of Moab, "but to this day no one knows the place of his burial" (Deut 34:6). Jude's quotation fills in details surrounding Moses' death and envisages a struggle between Michael and Satan over the body of Moses. Satan argued that Moses did not deserve burial because he had once killed an Egyptian (see Exod 2:12). Michael did not condemn Satan but simply said: "May the Lord rebuke you!" leaving judgment to the Lord. The point of this story is that the archangel Michael did not take on himself the power of passing judgment but left judgment to the Lord. Likewise, Jude says that God is the final judge and God will pass judgment on these intruding teachers.

Verses 10-13 Further examples of God's punishment

Jude turns now to consider the intruding teachers, who act like irrational animals (v. 10). They despise what they do not understand. Jude sees that their irrational attitudes will eventually lead to their own destruction (v. 10). Three more examples of sinners are taken from the biblical tradition and applied to the intruders (v. 11): Cain, Balaam, and Korah.

These false teachers are walking in *"the way of Cain"* (emphasis added). Cain murdered his brother Abel (Gen 4:8), so these intruding teachers are committing spiritual murder against the community.

winds, fruitless trees in late autumn, twice dead and uprooted. [13]They are like wild waves of the sea, foaming up their shameless deeds, wandering stars for whom the gloom of darkness has been reserved forever.

[14]Enoch, of the seventh generation from Adam, prophesied also about them when he said, "Behold, the Lord has come with his countless holy ones [15]to execute judgment on all and to convict everyone for all the godless deeds that they committed and for all the harsh words godless sinners have uttered against him." [16]These people are complainers, disgruntled ones who live

---

The intruders are also practicing *"Balaam's error"* (emphasis added). From references to Balaam in the book of Numbers (22–24; 25:1; 31:16-18), the implication emerges that Balaam led the Israelites into sin. In like manner these intruding teachers are leading the community that Jude addresses into sin.

Finally, *"the rebellion of Korah"* (emphasis added) refers to a revolt that Korah led against the authority of Moses and Aaron (Num 16). In like manner these intruding teachers are fomenting a rejection of Jude's authority and teaching. In the tradition these three examples symbolize those who lead the community into error and reject the duly appointed leaders of the community. These examples are certainly apt for the dangers these intruders pose to the community that Jude addresses.

Even the early Christian meals that remember the Lord's supper (called *agapai*, or "love feasts") have been infiltrated by these intruding teachers (v. 12). In graphic imagery, Jude uses four images drawn from nature (v. 12-13) to describe these intruding teachers. Common to these images is the concept that they do not act according to their nature. Instead they create chaos: "waterless clouds"; "fruitless trees"; "wild waves of the sea" splashing foam everywhere; and "wandering stars" (vv. 12-13). The implication for Jude's hearers/readers is clear: they are to avoid all contact with the intruding teachers because these teachers do not act according to the ways set by God. Instead they cause chaos by leading people astray.

Verses 14-19 Further warnings of judgment

Jude shows that the rise of these intruding teachers had been foretold in the past by both the prophets and the apostles. Jude refers to the example of Enoch (Gen 5:21-24), who was taken up to be with God without dying. He became an important figure in Jewish tradition between the testaments, as is seen from the influential apocryphal writing *1 Enoch.* Jude quotes from this writing to assure his hearers/readers that God will execute judgment on these intruding teachers: "Behold, the Lord has come

by their desires; their mouths utter bombast as they fawn over people to gain advantage.

Exhortations. ¹⁷But you, beloved, remember the words spoken beforehand by the apostles of our Lord Jesus Christ, ¹⁸for they told you, "In [the] last time there will be scoffers who will live according to their own godless desires." ¹⁹These are the ones who cause divisions; they live on the natural plane, devoid of the Spirit. ²⁰But you, beloved, build yourselves up in your most holy faith; pray in the holy Spirit. ²¹Keep yourselves in the love of God and wait for the mercy of our Lord Jesus Christ that leads to eternal life. ²²On those who waver, have mercy; ²³save others by snatching them out of the fire; on others have mercy with fear, abhorring even the outer garment stained by the flesh.

---

with his countless holy ones to execute judgment on all" (vv.14-15; see *1 Enoch* 1:9). This quotation lies closer to the text of *1 Enoch* discovered in Qumran than to other extant texts. The quotation's purpose is to stress the traditional teaching of divine judgment (Matt 16:27; 25:31-46).

Jude adds further support from Christian tradition by quoting a saying from the apostles: "In [the] last time there will be scoffers who will live according to their own godless desires" (v. 18). Since no such quotation appears in the rest of the New Testament, its origin must belong to the wider world of Christian tradition. The point of these references to *1 Enoch* and the apostles is clear: the presence of these intruding teachers was foretold in the past, and one can be certain that God's punishment and judgment await them.

Verses 20-23 Build up your faith

These verses present the climax of the letter. Jude spells out clearly why he has written them. He wants to build up the community's faith (v. 20). The way to accomplish this is through prayer in the Spirit, remaining in God's love, and relying upon Christ's mercy as they await the coming of the Lord (v. 21). For this reason they are to guard against the evil teachings of the intruders. It is not sufficient for the community and individuals to protect themselves from these false teachers.

While verses 22-23 contain a number of very difficult textual problems, nevertheless the basic meaning is clear: Jude reminds the members of his community of their responsibility to reach out to those who are wavering (v. 22) and "to save others by snatching them out of the fire" (v. 23). This is somewhat similar to the conclusion to the letter of James, where the hearers/readers are instructed that "whoever brings back a sinner from the error of his way will save his soul from death and will cover a multitude of sins" (Jas 5:20).

◄   **Doxology.** [24]To the one who is able to keep you from stumbling and to present you unblemished and exultant, in the presence of his glory, [25]to the only God, our savior, through Jesus Christ our Lord be glory, majesty, power, and authority from ages past, now, and for ages to come. Amen.

Verses 24-25 Final doxology

The letter concludes without any personal greetings so characteristic of Paul's letters. Instead, it ends with a hymn of praise (a doxology) in honor of God through Jesus Christ. God keeps the community from harm and brings them morally blameless into God's presence. This community praises this one God, the Savior, for God's glory, majesty, power, and authority that was in the past, is now, and will continue to be "for ages to come."

The Second Letter of Peter

Relationship between Second Peter and Jude

Virtually the whole of the letter of Jude is incorporated into Second Peter. Of Jude's twenty-five verses, no less than nineteen reappear in some form in Second Peter. A brief overview of this relationship can be seen from the following chart:

- 2 Peter 2:1-18 reproduce Jude 4-16
- 2 Peter 3:2-3 correspond to Jude 17-18
- 2 Peter 3:14 and 18 parallel Jude 24-25
- 2 Peter 1:1-2 echo Jude 1-2

That Second Peter used the letter of Jude appears evident from the above comparison. Second Peter is not an exact reproduction of Jude, but rather an adaptation and expansion. For example, the exclusion of the references to the apocryphal books of the *Assumption of Moses* and *1 Enoch* (Jude 9 and 14-15) is more easily understandable if we imagine the writer of Second Peter deliberately dropping Jude's references because they were not universally accepted as part of Scripture.

Author

This writing states that it is from "Symeon Peter, a slave and apostle of Jesus Christ" (1:1). The author is further acknowledged to be a witness to the transfiguration (1:16-18), implying that the author is Peter. There is also a reference to First Peter (3:1). Despite these indications, it is impossible to identify the author with the apostle Peter for the following reasons: (a) *The relationship between Second Peter and Jude:* Since Jude is a late writing and Second Peter has made use of Jude, Second Peter must be even later. (b) *There are also indications that the first generation of Christians had by now passed away:* "From the time when our ancestors fell asleep" (3:4). The writer belongs either to the second or third generation of Christians.

(c) *The writings of the apostle Paul have been made into a collection and are considered as Scripture:* ". . . beloved brother Paul, according to the wisdom given to him, also wrote to you, speaking of these things as he does *in all his letters.* In them there are some things hard to understand that the ignorant and unstable distort to their own destruction, just as they do *the other scriptures*" (2 Pet 3:15-16; emphasis added). (d) *Concern for the time of the second coming:* In the early decades after Jesus' death and resurrection, the first followers expected his imminent return (see 1 Cor 7:29-31). When this did not happen, the question of his return became increasingly important. We seem to be at a late period in the early church when the teaching regarding the Second Coming was under major attack.

This writing breathes an atmosphere that is at home at the end of the first century A.D. Since Peter died around A.D. 64, the apostle Peter could not have written it. As with First Peter, the author of Second Peter was probably one of Peter's disciples. He invoked Peter's authority to stress the traditional belief of the Christian faith and to correct the inroads of false teachers in areas and communities where the apostle Peter had originally taught. By invoking Peter's authority, he reminds his hearers/readers of Peter's teaching and speaks in the way Peter would have spoken in order to solve the problems these new teachers were raising. It is in this sense that this commentary refers to the author as Peter. It is best to see this letter coming from around the close of the first century or the beginning of the second century A.D.

Hearers/readers

The address is very "catholic," that is, universal: "To those who have received a faith of equal value to ours" (1:1). Since 3:1 refers to First Peter, perhaps the author is addressing the same readers in Asia Minor who are referred to in 1 Peter 1:1. It also presumes an audience that is very familiar with the writings of Paul and upholds Paul's authority (3:15-16). This indicates areas of Asia Minor where both Paul and Peter were active. The actual place of origin does not greatly matter, but since the author wrote in the name of Peter, he must have been associated with the same sphere of influence as Peter, probably Rome.

Literary form

The external form appears to be that of a letter (1:1-2). Instead of personal greetings at the end, the writing concludes with a brief doxology (3:18). Indications of a personal relationship between the sender and the recipients, so characteristic of a letter, are also lacking.

The literary form seems to be better suited to *the form of a testament*, a type of writing very popular in Christian and Jewish circles. The setting for a testament depicts someone who bids farewell to his intimate associates. He speaks about his imminent death and offers admonitions and edifying words, preparing them for calamities that are about to come when he departs. Examples of such testamentary farewell speeches abound throughout the biblical writings. The most characteristic of these are the speeches of Jacob (Gen 47:29–49:33); Moses (Deut 29–31); Joshua (Josh 23–24); and the twelve patriarchs (in the apocryphal writing *Testaments of the Twelve Patriarchs)*. In the Christian context there are the final farewell discourses of Jesus (John 13–17); and Paul (Acts 20:18-38). The writing of Second Timothy also falls into this category of a farewell testament. Since the characteristic features of a testament are all evident in this writing, it is justified in designating Second Peter as a "testament" or farewell speech that is sent (hence the letter form at the beginning) to encourage Christians to remain true to the teachings of the apostle Peter (and Paul) and to warn them against accepting the novel heresies that are currently being propagated.

The Second Letter of Peter

I. Address

Greeting. ¹Symeon Peter, a slave and apostle of Jesus Christ, to those who have received a faith of equal value to ours through the righteousness of our God and savior Jesus Christ: ²may grace and peace be yours in abundance through knowledge of God and of Jesus our Lord.

II. Exhortation to Christian Virtue

The Power of God's Promise. ³His ▶ divine power has bestowed on us

1:1-2 Greetings

The writing opens with the usual epistolary features naming the author, the recipients, and extending greetings. However, these are the only specific features of the letter format. The writer identifies himself as "Symeon Peter" (1:1), using the Semitic form of his name Symeon to remind the hearers/readers that he was one of the original followers of Jesus. This form Symeon also occurs in Acts 15:14. He is further identified as "a slave and apostle of Jesus Christ" (1:1). This designation shows his relationship to Jesus as his "slave" (see commentary on Jas 1:1) as well as his relationship to the spread of Christianity as an apostle.

The readers to whom this writing is addressed are not clearly defined: "to those who have received a faith of equal value to ours" (1:2). However, the writer stresses the essential equality between the faith of the apostles and that of the second- and third-generation Christians.

Finally, greetings are sent, using the phraseology of 1 Peter 1:2 "May grace and peace be yours in abundance." (Note a similar phrase in Jude 2: "May mercy, peace, and love be yours in abundance.") To this Second Peter adds the phrase "through knowledge of God and of Jesus our Lord" (1:2). As this is an important theme that is developed throughout this letter, it is intro-

---

▶ This symbol indicates a cross reference number in the *Catechism of the Catholic Church*. See page 76 for number citations.

Along the ragged shore of the Dead Sea,
53 miles long and 10 miles across at its widest point

everything that makes for life and devotion, through the knowledge of him who called us by his own glory and power. ⁴Through these, he has bestowed on us the precious and very great promises, so that through them you may come to share in the divine nature, after escaping from the corruption that is in the world because of evil desire. ⁵For this very reason, make every effort to supplement your faith with virtue, virtue with knowledge, ⁶knowledge with self-control, self-control with endurance, endurance with devotion, ⁷devotion with mutual affection, mutual affection with love. ⁸If these are yours and increase in abundance, they will keep you from being idle or un-

---

duced here at the beginning to draw the attention of the hearers/readers to this theme. Paul was also accustomed to use the opening greetings as a way of introducing important themes to his hearers/readers (see Rom 1:1-7).

1:3-4 Main theme announced

In place of the thanksgiving found in Paul's letters as well as Greco-Roman letters, Second Peter introduces the main ideas of this writing. God's power is the source and foundation for the Christian life. This power has communicated to believers everything they need for "life and devotion" (1:3). God has also bestowed great promises on believers (1:4), promises that are challenged by the opponents, especially those relating to the parousia (3:3-4). The whole purpose of God's promises is for believers to come "to share in the divine nature" after escaping the corruption of the world (1:4).

Second Peter is using vocabulary that is at home in the Hellenistic world to give expression to the work of God and of Christ. This shows that the writer seeks to express his thoughts in language that the Greco-Roman world would understand. This concept of sharing in the divine nature would be developed later in the writings of the church fathers to extol the concept of human divinization through the work of God and of Christ. Essentially, Second Peter is stating his theme that one overcomes the corrupting influence of this world through God's gift in Christ to share in God's nature.

1:5-11 Exhortation to remain firm in their call

The way of life of the believers is expressed through a number of virtues that the writer lists: faith, virtue, knowledge, self-control, endurance, devotion, mutual affection, love (1:5-7). The list begins with the virtue of faith and ends with love. The enumeration of virtues (and vices) was a popular way of presenting moral teaching in the Greco-Roman world. Paul reflects this mode of teaching well in his ethical instructions (e.g., Phil 4:8; 1 Tim 3:1-12). The positive exhortation is interrupted with

fruitful in the knowledge of our Lord Jesus Christ. ⁹Anyone who lacks them is blind and shortsighted, forgetful of the cleansing of his past sins. ¹⁰Therefore, brothers, be all the more eager to make your call and election firm, for, in doing so, you will never stumble. ¹¹For, in this way, entry into the eternal kingdom of our Lord and savior Jesus Christ will be richly provided for you.

Apostolic Witness. ¹²Therefore, I will always remind you of these things, even though you already know them and are established in the truth you have. ¹³I think it right, as long as I am in this "tent," to stir you up by a reminder, ¹⁴since I know that I will soon have to put it aside, as indeed our Lord Jesus Christ has shown me. ¹⁵I shall also make every effort to enable you always to remember these things after my departure.

¹⁶We did not follow cleverly devised myths when we made known to you the power and coming of our Lord Jesus

---

one negative note where the author warns that whoever does not strive to embrace these virtues is "blind and shortsighted" (1:9). This foreshadows one of the major concerns of this letter, namely, the false teachers who exemplify this spirit of blindness. For the writer, perseverance in remaining true to one's call is essential for the Christian (1:10-11).

1:12-15 Peter's testament

The writer speaks in the manner of the apostle Peter, who sees his death approaching (1:14). He wants to leave behind for his hearers/readers a reminder of what he had taught (1:15). This shows the nature of this present writing as a "testament," a very popular literary genre in the ancient world in which a famous person leaves behind a document that testifies to his enduring teaching (see Introduction, pp. 58–59). Perhaps, it would be best to identify Second Peter as a "testamentary letter." Here Peter, as the implied author, is aware that his death is imminent ("since I know that I will soon have to put it aside," 1:14). He refers to his human life as a "tent" (1:13), in the manner of Isaiah 38:12, which will be discarded in death. This letter, then, becomes a way in which Peter can remain with them after death: "I will always remind you of these things" (1:12); "to stir you up by a reminder" (1:13); "I shall also make every effort to enable you always to remember these things after my departure" (1:15).

1:16-21 Defense of prophecy concerning Jesus' second coming

In traditional testaments, reference to the leader's life would be given as an example for his hearers/readers. This section does exactly this by referring to events in Peter's life, such as being a witness to the transfiguration (1:17). This aspect of a testament will recur again in 3:1-3. This section gives attention to the major reason for this writing: to present Peter's de-

Christ, but we had been eyewitnesses of his majesty. [17]For he received honor and glory from God the Father when that unique declaration came to him from the majestic glory, "This is my Son, my beloved, with whom I am well pleased." [18]We ourselves heard this voice come from heaven while we were with him on the holy mountain. [19]Moreover, we possess the prophetic message that is altogether reliable. You will do well to be attentive to it, as to a lamp shining in a dark place, until day dawns and the morning star rises in your hearts. [20]Know this first of all, that there is no prophecy of scripture that is a matter of personal interpretation, [21]for no prophecy ever came through human will; but rather human beings moved by the holy Spirit spoke under the influence of God.

III. Condemnation of the False Teachers

False Teachers. [1]There were also false prophets among the people,

---

fense against false teachers. The traditional faith of the community is under attack. The essence of the attack relates to belief in Jesus' second coming (*parousia*). Peter defends his (and his fellow apostles') proclamation against two charges by the opponents: the second coming of Christ is a myth (1:16-18), and the prophecy of the second coming is not a true prophecy (1:20-21).

Second Peter denies both charges. In the first instance, the second coming in not based on "cleverly devised myths" (1:16), but on preaching that was based upon eyewitness experiences of God's own revelation when God testified to Jesus as God's own Son at the transfiguration (1:17). The appeal to the authority of the transfiguration serves as a defense for the teaching on the parousia (second coming). The transfiguration foreshadows the second coming of Jesus.

The second defense (1:20-21) concerns the truth of prophecy. The writer presents a memorable definition of biblical prophecy: ". . . *there is no prophecy of scripture that is a matter of personal interpretation, for no prophecy ever came through human will; but rather human beings moved by the holy Spirit spoke under the influence of God*" (1:20-21; emphasis added). For Second Peter, the interpretation of prophecy must rest upon a communal understanding rather than simply an individual feeling. The divine inspiration of the Hebrew Scriptures is clearly attested. The Hebrew prophets were divinely inspired witnesses to the coming of the Lord (1:21).

2:1-10a Defense against the false teachers

A characteristic feature of the genre of a testament is that a leader makes prophecies about the future. Second Peter presents the apostle Peter looking into the future and foreseeing the emergence of false teach-

just as there will be false teachers among you, who will introduce destructive heresies and even deny the Master who ransomed them, bringing swift destruction on themselves. ²Many will follow their licentious ways, and because of them the way of truth will be reviled. ³In their greed they will exploit you with fabrications, but from of old their condemnation has not been idle and their destruction does not sleep.

◄ **Lessons from the Past.** ⁴For if God did not spare the angels when they sinned, but condemned them to the chains of Tartarus and handed them over to be kept for judgment; ⁵and if he did not spare the ancient world, even though he preserved Noah, a herald of righteousness, together with seven others, when he brought a flood upon the godless world; ⁶and if he condemned the cities of Sodom and Gomorrah [to destruction], reducing them to ashes, making them an example for the godless [people] of what is coming; ⁷and if he rescued Lot, a righteous man oppressed by the licentious conduct of unprincipled people ⁸(for day after day that righteous man living among them was tormented in his righteous soul at the lawless deeds that he saw and heard), ⁹then the Lord knows how to rescue the devout from trial and to keep the unrighteous under punishment for the day of judgment, ¹⁰and especially those who follow the flesh

---

ers (2:1). While the characteristic of a testament was to present the prophecy (in this instance, the coming of false teachers) as an event to come in the future, it becomes clear from the rest of this chapter that these false teachers are already a problem within the community. The writer compares the false teachers that have appeared in their midst to the false prophets in the Hebrew Scriptures (2:1). The writer offers a long illustration from the Hebrew Scriptures to show how the wicked are punished and the righteous vindicated (2:4-10a).

This lays the groundwork for the argument that the future parousia brings with it reward and punishment (3:3-10). All the illustrations are taken from the letter of Jude. In fact, nineteen of Jude's twenty-five verses are taken over by Second Peter either in their entirety or in part (see Introduction, p. 57). In this section Second Peter makes use of Jude 4-8 and changes it in a number of ways. He puts all the examples from the Hebrew Scriptures in their chronological order as they appear in the Bible: rebellious angels, the flood, and Sodom and Gomorrah. In addition, Second Peter adds the two positive examples of Noah and Lot (2:5, 7-8) so that the hearer/reader sees clearly that God rewards those who stand up against false teachers. Second Peter argues this quite strongly in 2:9: just as God rescued the two righteous men (Noah and Lot) in the past and punished those who did evil (the rebellious angels, the people of Sodom and Gomorrah), so God will act in a similar way in the future. God will

with its depraved desire and show contempt for lordship.

False Teachers Denounced. Bold and arrogant, they are not afraid to revile glorious beings, ¹¹whereas angels, despite their superior strength and power, do not bring a reviling judgment against them from the Lord. ¹²But these people, like irrational animals born by nature for capture and destruction, revile things that they do not understand, and in their destruction they will also be destroyed, ¹³suffering wrong as payment for wrongdoing. Thinking daytime revelry a delight, they are stains and defilements as they revel in their deceits while carousing with you. ¹⁴Their eyes are full of adul-

---

rescue "the devout" and punish "the unrighteous" (2:9), namely, those who do evil, identified later as the false teachers.

2:10b-16 Denunciation of the false teachers

The writer points out how the false teaching gives rise to an evil way of life. Again, most of this material comes from the letter of Jude 8-16 and is adapted to suit Second Peter's context. The first example (2:10b-11) concerns reviling "glorious beings," that is, the angels. The false teachers deny that the angels have any influence on humanity. Second Peter leaves out Jude's example of Michael and Satan because it does not fit his context. According to the understanding of the time, one of the roles of angels was to report to God about the actions of human beings (see Job 1:6-12). The angels should by rights have brought accusations against the false teachers before God's throne, but they did not do so (2:11).

The second example (2:12-14) shows how the immoral lives of the false teachers reflect the lives of animals rather than human beings (2:12). Second Peter seeks to warn his hearers/readers against any association with these false teachers, since they draw others into their evil ways (2:14).

The final example in this section is that of Balaam (2:15-16, taken from Jude 11). For Second Peter, the example of Balaam illustrates a false prophet who strayed from the true message. Even his donkey rebuked him (2:16; see Num 22:23-35). Balaam becomes a further example to the hearers/readers of the punishment of an evildoer.

2:17-22 Further denunciations

Second Peter accuses his opponents of being people who lack direction. They act like "waterless springs and mists driven by a gale" (2:17). In the first instance, Second Peter shows the harmful effects these false teachers have on others (2:17-19). Again the writer is relying upon Jude 12-13, 16. The effect of their teaching is to seduce Christians, especially those who have recently converted from paganism: "Those who have barely es-

tery and insatiable for sin. They seduce unstable people, and their hearts are trained in greed. Accursed children! [15]Abandoning the straight road, they have gone astray, following the road of Balaam, the son of Bosor, who loved payment for wrongdoing, [16]but he received a rebuke for his own crime: a mute beast spoke with a human voice and restrained the prophet's madness.

[17]These people are waterless springs and mists driven by a gale; for them the gloom of darkness has been reserved. [18]For, talking empty bombast, they seduce with licentious desires of the flesh those who have barely escaped from people who live in error. [19]They promise them freedom, though they themselves are slaves of corruption, for a person is a slave of whatever overcomes him. [20]For if they, having escaped the defilements of the world through the knowledge of [our] Lord and savior Jesus Christ, again become entangled and overcome by them, their last condition is worse than their first. [21]For it would have been better for them not to have known the way of righteousness than after knowing it to turn back from the holy commandment handed down to them. [22]What is expressed in the true proverb has happened to them, "The dog returns to its own vomit," and "A bathed sow returns to wallowing in the mire."

---

caped from people who live in error." (2:18). Second Peter shows the consequences of what happens when belief in the second coming of Christ is denied together with belief in reward and punishment at the last day. Since there is no final judgment, they give themselves over to a life that knows no restrictions, as is seen in leading a life devoted to the "licentious desires of the flesh" (2:18).

Second Peter then considers how the teaching of the false teachers harms themselves (2:20-22). When they became Christians, they "escaped the defilements of the world through the knowledge of [our] Lord and savior Jesus Christ" (2:20). Now their teaching has drawn them back, and their situation is worse than it was previously (2:21).

Finally, the author uses two well-known parables to arouse revulsion in the minds of his hearers/readers: he compares these false teachers to a dog that returns to its own vomit and to a sow that returns to wallow in mud (2:22). The first proverb comes from Proverbs 26:11: "As the dog returns to his vomit, / so the fool repeats his folly." In the world of the first century, a dog was not the well-received, domesticated animal of today. A "dog" was generally a word used to insult someone. So the two animals (dog and sow) would evoke the same feelings of revulsion in the hearers/readers. The source of the second proverb is unknown; it was probably a traditional proverb found in their culture.

IV. The Delay of
the Second Coming

3 **Denial of the Parousia.** ¹This is now, beloved, the second letter I am writing to you; through them by way of reminder I am trying to stir up your sincere disposition, ²to recall the words previously spoken by the holy prophets and the commandment of the Lord and savior through your apostles. ³Know this first of all, that in the last days scoffers will come [to] scoff, living according to their own desires ⁴and saying, "Where is the promise of his coming? From the time when our ancestors fell asleep, everything has remained as it was from the beginning of creation." ⁵They deliberately ignore the fact that the heavens existed of old and earth was formed out of water and through water by the word of God; ⁶through these the world that then existed was destroyed, deluged with water. ⁷The present heavens and earth have been reserved by the same word

3:1-10 Defense regarding the delay of the parousia

The writer opens this passage in a formal way (3:1-2), reminding the faithful of Peter's authority. It is also a reminder of the genre of a testament. He deliberately associates this writing with First Peter by identifying it as his "second letter" (3:1). As with a testament, this letter serves to take the place of Peter's physical presence among them. A further dimension of the genre of a testament is found in the rest of this passage, where the writer, using the figure of Peter, looks into the future and speaks about these false teachers who are to come (3:3), a vision that has now been realized within the community.

This section considers the heart of the opponents' teaching. The writer begins with a call to remember the tradition, particularly the teachings both of the prophets and of Jesus, whose message his apostles handed on (3:2). Previously the false teachers had accused Peter of inventing myths (1:16). Second Peter again reiterates that his teaching is based upon the word of Christ passed on through the apostles (3:2). He spells out clearly the heart of the opponents' rejection: the return of Christ (3:4). The question "Where is the promise of his coming?" (3:4) is a typical biblical question, implying doubt and derision on the part of the one asking the question (see also Judg 6:13; Isa 36:19).

The basis for the opponents' objections rests on the perceived permanence of the world: "From the time when our ancestors fell asleep, everything has remained as it was from the beginning of creation" (3:4). They claim that God has not been actively involved in the world, so why should God begin now? To this Peter gives a number of responses taken from biblical history:

for fire, kept for the day of judgment and of destruction of the godless.

⁸But do not ignore this one fact, beloved, that with the Lord one day is like a thousand years and a thousand years like one day. ⁹The Lord does not delay his promise, as some regard "delay," but he is patient with you, not wishing that any should perish but that all should come to repentance. ¹⁰But the day of the Lord will come like a thief, and then the heavens will pass away with a mighty roar and the elements will be dissolved by fire, and the earth and everything done on it will be found out.

Exhortation to Preparedness. ¹¹Since everything is to be dissolved in this way, what sort of persons ought [you] to be,

---

- By God's word, the creation occurred and earth was formed from water (3:5; see Gen 1:9-10). The concept that all things were derived from water as the original element was also a Greek philosophical understanding.
- By God's word, the world was destroyed by water (3:6; see Gen 7:4).
- By God's word, the earth and everything on it will be destroyed by fire (3:7; the biblical roots of this belief in the destruction of the world by fire are found in late Hebrew writings such as Isaiah 66:15-16 and Malachi 3:19. The source for this biblical view is probably to be traced back to the Persians.)
- The delay in the parousia only appears to be a delay from the human perspective. With God time does not matter: "With the Lord one day is like a thousand years and a thousand years like one day" (3:8; this saying finds its origin in Psalm 90:4).
- The delay is actually a sign of God's patience, making it possible for more people to repent (3:9). This statement is a deduction from the very definition of God as a God of mercy and compassion (Exod 34:6).
- Finally, as Jesus predicted in Mark 13:32-37, the day of the Lord will come unexpectedly, like a thief in the night (3:10).

Second Peter rests his argument on the understanding that since the world has already undergone change through the power of God's word (in the creation and in the flood), so too it is to experience change in the future with the return of Jesus and a final judgment. While the end of the world is a certainty, Second Peter (as with the rest of the New Testament) gives no speculation on when this will occur.

3:11-13 Consequences of this teaching

Because the world will end in such a cataclysmic way, the readers should lead lives that strive after "holiness and devotion" (3:11). This call is set within the context of apocalyptic language that sees the destruction

conducting yourselves in holiness and devotion, ¹²waiting for and hastening the coming of the day of God, because of which the heavens will be dissolved in flames and the elements melted by fire. ¹³But according to his promise we await new heavens and a new earth in which righteousness dwells.

¹⁴Therefore, beloved, since you await these things, be eager to be found with- out spot or blemish before him, at peace. ¹⁵And consider the patience of our Lord as salvation, as our beloved brother Paul, according to the wisdom given to him, also wrote to you, ¹⁶speaking of these things as he does in all his letters. In them there are some things hard to understand that the ignorant and un- stable distort to their own destruction, just as they do the other scriptures.

of the world (3:12) and the emergence of "new heavens and a new earth" (3:13). This description of the destruction of the world by means of fire is found only here in the New Testament; nevertheless, it was a common cultural view of the first century A.D.

3:14-16 Even Paul agrees with this teaching

Second Peter appeals to Paul's letters for support, since Paul taught the same things that Second Peter is teaching. Paul taught that there would be a judgment of all at the end of time (Rom 14:10-12). Paul also envisaged the delay of judgment as a time for repentance (Rom 2:4-5). In appealing to Paul's support, Second Peter makes three important observations. He un- derstands that Paul was inspired in the writing of his letters ("according to the wisdom given to him," 3:15). Secondly, he shows that there was a tend- ency within the early church to collect Paul's letters ("in all his letters," 3:16). Thirdly, Paul's letters are considered to have an authority equal to that of the Hebrew Scriptures ("the other scriptures," 3:16). Consequently, the hearers/readers can rely on this teaching concerning the parousia, since it is the traditional teaching of the church, and the two greatest apostles, Paul and Peter, also bear witness to this traditional belief.

3:17-18 Final exhortation and doxology

The writer makes a final appeal to his hearers/readers to be on guard against the deceptions of the false teachers (3:17). He addresses his hear- ers/readers as "beloved" (3:17), a term that he had used frequently throughout this final chapter (3:1, 8, 14). In a positive way, he returns to his opening statement (1:2), where he encouraged his readers to grow in the "knowledge of God and of Jesus our Lord." This final appeal reminds the reader of the importance of the traditional teaching and knowledge about Jesus and his preaching, especially as it relates to his second coming and the end of the world: You can be sure that Jesus Christ will return. Fi-

V. Final Exhortation
and Doxology

[17]Therefore, beloved, since you are forewarned, be on your guard not to be led into the error of the unprincipled and to fall from your own stability. [18]But grow in grace and in the knowledge of our Lord and savior Jesus Christ. To him be glory now and to the day of eternity. [Amen.]

---

nally, Second Peter ends with a doxology in praise of the Lord Jesus Christ. This praise is meant to be addressed to Jesus from now until eternity (3:18).

REVIEW AIDS AND DISCUSSION TOPICS

The Letter of James

1. Identify the author of this letter. What was his position in the early church? To whom is the letter addressed? What was the purpose of this letter (pp. 7, 11)?

2. Identify three or four major themes that are threaded throughout this letter (pp. 12–16). Are any or all of these important in your life today? Explain.

3. Define the virtue of wisdom (p. 13). Is wisdom a virtue one acquires through study and good works or is wisdom a gift of God? Identify some of the characteristics of someone you consider a wise person.

4. What phrase in the first chapter might summarize the whole letter of James (p. 15)? Why is this directive so important to James?

5. What does James say about showing favoritism? To whom is he addressing his admonition (pp. 16–17)? How does this resonate with your own behavior? Give examples of how the church, your parish, or other organizations in your community defer to or honor the wealthy.

6. What does James mean when he asks, "What good is it, if someone says he has faith but does not have works" (pp. 18–19)? How does this differ from Martin Luther's doctrine of justification by faith? What impact did this disparity have on the church and how does it affect us today?

7. What is James's warning to teachers (p. 20)? Does his admonishment about judging teachers more strictly apply today? Explain.

8. What were the causes of division when James wrote this letter? What causes divisions in families, neighborhoods, communities today?

9. James deals with the subject of wealth and pride at least twice in his letter. What is his concern about the wealthy? Chapter 5 is specifically addressed to what group? How do we relate to this caution today (pp. 13, 24, 25)?

10. What role models does James give us for enduring hardship with patience (p. 26)? Identify modern prophets who have helped you to persevere in your faith.

11. Why is the theme of prayer such an appropriate ending for the letter of James (pp. 27–28)?

The First Letter of Peter

1. Are we certain this letter was written by Peter? Why or why not (p. 29)? Who may have written the letter? To whom is the letter written (pp. 30, 31)?

2. What are the major themes in this letter (pp. 33, 37, 45)?

3. The author of First Peter reminds his readers what the Old Testament prophets said regarding salvation. Why is this important (p. 34)?

4. What, according to First Peter, does it mean to be holy (p. 35)? Can you identify holy people in your life today? Have you heard a homily on holiness recently?

5. How is the theme of 1 Peter 2 related to the Passover motif? Explain the parallels.

6. Reflect on how the author in 2:4-8 uses the metaphors of a living stone and of a stumbling block (pp. 36–37). Of what value are these metaphors in our understanding of First Peter? Think of other metaphors that could be used to illustrate the point of this passage.

7. "Be subject to every human institution for the Lord's sake" (2:13). Why was this important in the early Church (p. 38)? How do we respond to this exhortation in the twenty-first century? How do we explain our response?

8. Why must we remember the time and setting of First Peter when reading the instructions to slaves, wives, and husbands (pp. 39–40)? How can we translate these directives so as to be meaningful today? Give examples.

9. First Peter challenges Christians to be ready to witness to their faith (p. 42). Give examples of how this is done in our twenty-first-century society. Can you think of persons who, in your lifetime, have suffered persecution for their faith?

10. How do Christians participate in Christ's death and resurrection (p. 43)?

11. The author of First Peter believes the end of the world is near (pp. 44–45). What does he admonish his readers to do in preparation for the end? How do you respond to those who forecast the end of the world on a specific day and year?

12. Suffering is a theme woven through First Peter. Why should suffering be a cause for rejoicing? How do we accept suffering that we experience today?

The Letter of Jude

1. Identify the author of the letter. What is known about the author? To whom is this letter addressed (pp. 48–49)?

2. What references or examples does Jude use to remind his readers of those who lost favor with God and were punished (p. 52)?

3. Who are the "intruding teachers" in Jude's letter? According to Jude, what are their wrongdoings and what is their destiny (p. 53)? Can you identify "intruding teachers" living today? How are we to relate to such teachers?

4. What graphic images does Jude use to describe the intruding teachers (p. 54)?

5. How does Jude suggest his readers protect themselves from the false teachings of the intruders (p. 55)? How do we today protect ourselves from false teachings?

6. How does Jude propose to his readers that they build up their faith? What does he challenge them to do for those who are wavering in their faith (p. 55)? How do you respond to this challenge today?

The Second Letter of Peter

1. What do we know about the author of Second Peter? Why might this letter be designated as a testament? To whom is Second Peter addressed (pp. 58–59)?

2. What is the main theme of Second Peter (p. 62)? Does this have relevance for us today?

3. In presenting moral teaching, Second Peter uses a list of several virtues that believers must have (p. 62). How meaningful are any or all of these virtues to you in your own life?

4. Define *parousia*. What do the false teachers preach about the parousia? How does Second Peter defend the parousia (p. 64)?

5. Compare 2 Peter 2–3 with Jude 4-19. Who is "borrowing" from whom? Discuss similarities in content and style.

6. Second Peter 2:17-22 uses harsh words to describe the false teachers (pp. 66–67). Can you paraphrase this passage to make it relevant to the false teachers we hear on radio and television, or read in the tabloids today?

7. How does 2 Peter defend the Second Coming against the arguments of the false teachers regarding Jesus' promise of his return (pp. 68–69)? How would you defend Jesus' Second Coming to a non-believer today?

8. What does 2 Peter 3:10 say about how the world will end (p. 69)? Have there been such momentous catastrophes in your lifetime that would lead you to think the world was coming to an end? 9/11; tsunami; Hurricane Katrina? others?

9. How are the letters of Paul used to support the teachings of Second Peter (p. 70)?

10. Reflect on the final exhortation of Second Peter (pp. 70–71). Of what significance is this to you today?

INDEX OF CITATIONS FROM THE
CATECHISM OF THE CATHOLIC CHURCH

The arabic number(s) following the citation refer to the paragraph number(s) in the *Catechism of the Catholic Church*. The asterisk following a paragraph number indicates that the citation has been paraphrased.

James

1:5-8	2633*, 2737*
1:13	2846
1:14-15	2847*
1:17	212, 2642
1:25	1972*
1:27	2208
2:7	432,* 2148
2:10-11	2069,* 2079*
2:10	578
2:12	1972*
2:14-26	162*
2:15-16	2447
2:26	1815
4:1-10	2737*
4:2-3	2737
4:4	2737
4:5	2737
5:1-6	2445
5:4	1867,* 2409,* 2434*
5:12	2153*
5:14-15	1510, 1511,* 1526
5:14	1519
5:15	1519,* 1520
5:16	2737*
5:16b-18	2582
5:20	1434*

1 Peter

1	2627*
1:3-9	2627*
1:3	654*
1:7	1031*
1:10-12	719
1:18-20	602
1:18-19	517*
1:18	622
1:19	613*
1:23	1228,* 2769
2:1-10	2769*
2:1	2475
2:4-5	1141,* 1179
2:4	552
2:5	756,* 901, 1268, 1330,* 1546*
2:7	756*
2:9	709,* 782, 803, 1141, 1268, 1546*
2:13-17	1899*
2:13	2238
2:16	2238
2:21	618
2:24	612
3:1-7	2204*
3:9	1669*
3:18-19	632*

3:20-21	845*
3:20	1219
3:21	128,* 1094,* 1794*
4:6	634
4:7	670,* 1806
4:8	1434
4:14	693
4:17	672*
5:3	893, 1551*
5:4	754*
5:7	322
5:8	409,* 2849*

Jude

3	171
24-25	2641*

2 Peter

1:3-4	1996*
1:4	406, 1129,* 1265, 1692, 1721, 1812*
1:16-18	554*
2:4	392*
3:9	1037, 2822
3:11-12	671*
3:12-13	677*
3:13	1043, 1405*